T5-BPY-566

KNOWLEDGE
ITS VALUES AND LIMITS

GUSTAVE WEIGEL, S. J.
ARTHUR G. MADDEN

GREENWOOD PRESS, PUBLISHERS
WESTPORT, CONNECTICUT

The Library of Congress has catalogued this publication as follows:

Library of Congress Cataloging in Publication Data

Weigel, Gustave, 1906-1964.
  Knowledge; its values and limits.

  Original ed. issued as no. S-16 of A spectrum
book.
  Bibliography: p.
  1. Knowledge, Theory of. 2. Thought and thinking.
3. Certainty. I. Madden, Arthur G., joint author.
II. Title.
[BD161.W36 1973]   121   72-10722
ISBN 0-8371-6627-6

IMPRIMI POTEST

> Joannes M. Daley, S.J.
> *Praep. Prov. Marylandiae*

NIHIL OBSTAT

> Edward A. Cerny, S.S.
> *Censor Librorum*

IMPRIMATUR

> ✠ Francis P. Keough, D.D.
> *Archbishop of Baltimore*
> *March 7, 1961*

The *Nihil Obstat* and *Imprimatur* are official declarations that a book or pamphlet is free of doctrinal or moral error. No implication is contained therein that those who have granted the *Nihil Obstat* and *Imprimatur* agree with the contents, opinions, or statements expressed.

© *1961 by Prentice-Hall, Inc., Englewood Cliffs, N. J.*

All rights reserved

Originally published in 1961
by Prentice-Hall, Inc., Englewood Cliffs, N. J.

Reprinted with the permission
of Prentice-Hall, Inc.

First Greenwood Reprinting 1973

Library of Congress Catalogue Card Number 72-10722

ISBN 0-8371-6627-6

Printed in the United States of America

KNOWLEDGE

Eminent theologian and philosopher Gustave Wei-
gel, S.J. (Ph.D. and S.T.D., Gregorian University,
Rome) has lectured extensively both here and
abroad. A prominent author and lecturer, Father
Weigel is Professor of Ecclesiology at Woodstock
College, School of Divinity. His numerous works
include *A Survey of Protestant Theology in Our
Time, Faith and Understanding in America,* and
American Dialogue (with Robert McAfee Brown).
He is the holder of the 1960 Christian Wisdom
Medal awarded by Loyola University of Chicago.

Arthur G. Madden, co-author of the volume, holds
a Ph.D. from Fordham University. A teacher of
many years' experience, he is Chairman of the
Division of Philosophy at Mount Saint Agnes College in Maryland.

BD
161
W36

Preface

This small volume is presented as an essay on the values and limits of human thought and in particular of two kinds of disciplined thought, science and philosophy. It does not pretend to be a treatise exhaustive of the subject. It simply intends to describe the more commonly recognized forms of knowledge and to make a critical evaluation of them. Some historical material has been given in order to show how the problems involved in human knowledge came to the attention of philosophers and how certain of the philosophers came to grips with the problems. It is hoped that, both to those who are formally engaged in the study of philosophy and to the educated reading public at large, this book will be a stimulus to engage in some serious thinking about thought. The fact that the truth-value of our knowledge is basic not only for our theoretical conceptions of reality but also for our personal commitments in the various areas of human conduct should make the subject of prime concern to all.

The text is based on lectures on theory of knowledge given by Father Weigel during the years 1950-1956 at Fordham University Graduate School as part of a cycle of courses concerned with epistemology, metaphysics, and religion.* The material has been edited and additions made by Dr. Madden.

We are indebted to John G. Marzolf, S.J., for reading the section on science and for his constructive criticisms, and to

---

* The other parts of this cycle which concerned the nature of religion and of religious knowledge and examined the presuppositions of the philosophical proofs for the existence of God are being published in a companion volume entitled: *Religion and the Knowledge of God.*

v

168104

Dean R. Haggard of Loyola College for his comments on some mathematical points. We wish to thank Mary Nicholson Madden for her part in the typing of the manuscript and for some suggested corrections and Jane Carlon Cox for her expert assistance in proofreading. Our thanks go also to the Yale University Press, the Cambridge University Press, and to the Estate of Albert Einstein for permission to quote from their publications.

Contents

1

The Problems of Knowledge

The Questioning of Our Knowledge

That human knowledge presents many problems is evident even to the least reflective man of "common sense." Although he has a deep-seated spontaneous confidence in his ability to achieve the truth, he is on occasions mildly irritated by his own errors and more frequently shocked by the errors of others. He is happy when he is certain that his knowledge is true, unhappy when he is in doubt. The discovery that his certainty has been proved now and again to be unwarranted is perplexing. From these experiences he comes to realize that things are not always as he perceives them, that his conceptions of things are often wrong, that he and his fellows make mistakes in reasoning, and that his moral and aesthetic judgments are sometimes contradicted by others. Despite the scandal of error and the disagreements among men, the pragmatic value of his knowledge in meeting his daily needs is sufficient to sustain his faith in the knowledge enterprise. Lack of interest or absorption in the business of living and earning a living keeps him from entering upon a really critical examination of the values and limits of his knowledge.

The critical examination of knowledge, however, has been an important task of philosophers from the very beginning. In their earliest attempts to comprehend the nature of reality they were confronted with the problems of knowledge, for it is only within the limits of our knowledge that we can grasp the real. The field of philosophy which makes this study is called epistemology, a somewhat awesome Greek derivative. *Epistéme* in Greek means knowledge, and, in philosophical jargon, *logos* means a reflective treatment of the subject to which it is referred. Hence all that *epistemology* says is a reflective treatment of knowledge. Most people feel about epistemology as they feel about snakes: terribly fascinated but fearful of coming too close. Such an attitude is hardly helpful, nor is it justified in fact. Snakes may bite but knowledge will not. The reason that most people are terrified by epistemology is the illusiveness of the object under consideration and the vast quantity of work that has been done in the field. A brief review of the investigations of some philosophers to whom the epistemological problem was of prime importance will introduce us to the nature of knowledge and to some of the questions raised about it.

Historical Review of Some Theories of Knowledge

Some epistemological meditation was implicit in the work of the first Greek philosophers, Thales, Anaximander, Anaximenes, and Heraclitus. These men were trying to find the common base of reality. Now it is obvious to the smallest child that reality as it presents itself to our observation is chaotically pluralistic. The philosophy dominant in the mid-twentieth century, existentialism, insists on this truth. Therefore, the first philosophers who observed reality, no less than the existentialist, took an epistemological stand when they sought for the basic form of the real. Such a basic form *cannot be observed,* and that means that they were appealing to knowledge on some level other than that of common sense observation. Such an appeal supposes some thinking about thought. With these early physicists, as they were called, mathematics entered the field. Now mathematical thinking is an epistemological commitment, for, as in the case of the common basis of reality, the objects of the mathematician's investigation are not observable by sense experience.

The skepticism of the Sophists, which is itself an epistemological stand, spurred Socrates and Plato to the first intensive study of the differences in the kinds of knowledge and their objective referents. In the teaching of Plato the objects of our sense perceptions are the individual, contingent, changing things of the material world. Our perceptions of these cannot give us true knowledge because true knowledge is of that which *is,* whereas sense objects are in constant flux or becoming. True knowledge (*epistéme*) is of the stable and the necessary and this is given to us in our universal concepts, the objective referents of which are the absolute, unchanging Forms or Ideas which have a reality transcending the individual objects or events of our experience. The individuals in some way reflect or participate in the Forms and to that extent give us knowledge, but of a less perfect kind (*doxa,* opinion) than our knowledge of the Forms. The Forms, and in particular the highest Form, the Good, are the ground of the reality and intelligibility of individual objects and also the ultimate standards of human conduct.

Plato's pupil, Aristotle, disagreed with his master on the origin of our universal concepts and the nature of the realities to which they referred. In Plato's doctrine the universal concept is an intuition of an intelligible reality. For Aristotle the concept is a construction on the part of the mind by a process called abstraction, in which the mind focuses upon the essence or immanent form of the individual to the exclusion of everything which individuates. This essence can be common to many. The ontological basis, i.e., the basis in reality, of the universal concept is not, as for Plato, the transcendent Form or Idea, but the similarity of forms existing in the many individuals of our experience. Thus for Aristotle in his mature period, the forms are immanent in the world of our sense experience; there is no separate world of Platonic Forms.

The materialism of the Stoics and Epicureans led them to reject both the Platonic intuition of Ideas and the Aristotelian abstraction of the immanent forms for an epistemology based on the sense perception of singulars. This was not without its difficulties for the Stoics who, in returning to the cosmology of Heraclitus, emphasized a universal natural law as the immanent operation of Reason in the material world. To their sensism they added an intellectualism of general concepts, some of which are virtually innate, others developed out of sense experience. By these general concepts man's reason comes to know the universal laws of nature.

Along with the rise and development of Stoicism and Epicureanism came a wave of skepticism which lasted well into the Christian period. The counter-attack on skepticism was made by the Neo-Platonists. In both Plotinus and Saint Augustine we find that the finite and sensible reality is not intelligible except as measured against an absolute norm. The knowledge of these absolute norms comes, according to Saint Augustine, by means of a divine illumination, whereby we have an intuition of the eternal, unchanging, intelligible realities which are the divine Ideas.

The Augustinian epistemology together with the Aristotelian revival in the Christian era produced the prolonged debate among medieval philosophers on the nature of universals. The question was asked: is the universal prior to the individual (*universale ante rem*), is it in the individual (*universale in re*), or is it merely a human construction in the form of a mere concept or word (*universale post rem*)? The label of extreme realism has been given to those who held the Platonic position or variations of it, to the effect that universals have a reality prior to individuals. Those who maintained that the universal, though strictly a conceptual construction, existed fundamentally in individuals have been called moderate realists. Those who looked upon universals as mere human devices have been called conceptualists or nominalists, the former if they considered the universal as a construct of the mind with no correlate in the individuals, the latter if they considered it simply as a name or word which we adopt in order to handle many individuals with convenience and economy.[1]

The controversy over universals points up two tendencies that have appeared in philosophy from its beginnings, having been underlined early by Heraclitus in his contrast between sense experience and the *logos* or reason. One is empiricism which emphasizes knowledge through sense experience; the other is rationalism which stresses man's tendency to conceptualize or universalize. The latter involves the a priori aspects of knowledge, i.e., knowledge which is independent of and logically prior to experience. These two poles of knowledge became more and more opposed in modern philosophy.

It was reserved for the modern period beginning with Descartes to make a thoroughly systematic examination of human knowledge. Skepticism resulting from the disagreements of philosophers, the rise of the new science to challenge the Aristotelian conception of the world, the trend to empiricism, and the extension of mathematics called for a reassessment of what men can know with certainty. Descartes was impressed with the certainty of the propositions in a mathematical system and with the possibility of weaving a complete system of knowledge from a few definitions and axioms. He felt that all knowledge could be worked out by a mathematical method after starting with some self-evident data. He approached the task with the instrument of methodic doubt which called into question every proposition about which any doubt could be raised. His aim was to find the self-evident, undeniable data from which as a base he could then infer all other propositions

---

[1] Labels, however convenient, often do an injustice to a particular philosopher. Moreover, the overtones of the label depend on who invents it or who is applying it.

with certainty. His starting point he finds in the affirmation of his conscious states and in the affirmation of his existence: *Cogito, ergo sum;* I think, therefore I am. As to the objective referents of these conscious states he cannot at first be certain because, to use Descartes' own extravagant supposition, men may be subject to a malignant genius which is bent on deceiving them. But of their existence as subjective states there can be no doubt for Descartes because of their self-evidence, their clearness and distinctness. Since he finds as a content of consciousness a clear idea of a Perfect Being, Descartes concludes by an ontological argument among others that a Perfect Being, God, exists. God is then called as the guarantor that an external world of extended objects exists, for an infinitely perfect Creator would not implant in us the clear idea of extended objects distinct from a thinking substance, only to deceive us. The intrinsic validity of man's senses and reason are entailed in the veracity of God.

This limiting of the date of consciousness to the subjective pole introduced into modern philosophy the "closed consciousness" with its consequent theory of representative ideas. According to this theory the direct and immediate object of the mind is an idea that stands as an intermediary between the mind and the real object. This doctrine was fundamental in the epistemology of John Locke. In opposition to Descartes, Locke denied that we have innate ideas and maintained that all knowledge is derived from experience. He accepted as incontrovertible data our sensations and our reflections upon them but believed that the existence of an external world is attained by inference. Locke's views of substance and qualities are of interest in connection with our knowledge of ourselves and of objects other than ourselves. Substance, says Locke, is some sort of substratum or support of qualities, which substratum we assume to exist since it is difficult to believe that qualities exist by themselves or of themselves form consistent groupings. In this view substance is an unknown x; what is known is the complex of qualities. Sense qualities are of two kinds. The primary qualities, such as solidity, extension, and motion, are really in the objects as we perceive them. The secondary qualities, such as color, sound, and taste, are proper to only one sense and are strictly affections of the knowing subject, although caused by some power in the object.

The difficulty of getting from the representative idea to the inferred object was recognized by George Berkeley, who rejected the existence of material substances independent of our perceptions. For Berkeley, to be is to be perceived. The only substances are minds, the infinite mind of God and the finite minds of creatures. Primary and secondary sense qualities alike are affections of the mind as given us by God who is the Author of the consistent system of sense data. This is complete immaterialism.

David Hume went beyond the position of Berkeley. He, too, rejects representative ideas in denying that we can know any substance, material or immaterial, to which the data can be referred. Even the self is nothing but a series of sense data which are habitually grouped together by the psychological laws of association. The data are always perceived as separate and distinct. No real relation of one datum to another is ever experienced and hence the various groupings must be explained psychologically by the habit of association. Both Berkeley and Hume denied abstract concepts and adopted a nominalistic position on universals.

The radical empiricism of Hume and its attendant skepticism aroused Immanuel Kant to a new consideration of the nature of knowledge. Hume's epistemology made science and philosophy impossible as knowledge of the real since these are concerned with that which is universal and necessary, neither of which characteristics is given in sense experience.

Kant puts the question: how is science possible? How can it be concerned with the individual objects of the world of sense experience and yet possess a universal validity? In giving the answer to this question Kant distinguishes judgments according to whether they are analytic or synthetic, and a priori or a posteriori. An analytic judgment is one whose predicate is implied in the subject and is revealed by an analysis of the meaning of the subject. A synthetic judgment has a predicate with a content that goes beyond the mere definition of the subject concept. "Man is rational" is an example of an analytic judgment since the predicate "rational" states what is already contained in the concept of "man." On the other hand, "Some men are wealthy" is a synthetic proposition since the predicate "wealthy" is not implied in the concept "man." Likewise, "hydrogen is combustible" is a synthetic proposition. An a priori proposition is a universal judgment, the universal and necessary character of which is not given in experience but is independent of and logically prior to experience. An a posteriori judgment is one based solely on experience. "Man is mortal" is a priori because its universal and necessary character is not given in experience. "John is eating dinner" is a posteriori because the truth of the judgment depends on empirical evidence. Scientific knowledge, says Kant, is synthetic a priori. It is a combination of an empirical content and a rational form. The universal and necessary character is contributed by the conceptualizing power of the mind. Concepts without percepts are empty; percepts without concepts are blind.

Kant describes the process as taking place on two levels, the level of sense perception and that of the understanding. The raw material of knowledge is given in experience in the form of sense data. Even these sense data do not give us the objects as individuals but must be molded by the innate, a priori forms of sensibility, namely, space and time. This dynamic process on the part of the mind produces the percept or phenomenon, i.e., the object as it is made to appear to us by the structure of the mind. Then, on the level of the understanding, the phenomena are stamped with the innate, a priori, logical categories, such as substance, causality, and relation, which are also part of the structure of the mind. Thus, although experience presents us with the matter of our knowledge, the mind imposes the form and gives it the universal and necessary quality. Things as they are in themselves (noumena) remain unknowable; only the phenomena are known.

Kant's critique ushered in a period of idealism culminating in the absolutism of Hegel. Against this absolutism and its absorption of the individual, Kierkegaard rebelled by bringing forth his form of existentialism, which no one listened to in his time. Positivism overcame idealism and scientism overcame positivism. Now in the twentieth century Ernst Cassirer has made his great contribution in four volumes. In the introduction to the last of these volumes, *The Problem of Knowledge: Philosophy, Science and History since Hegel,* Cassirer states:

> Never before in the history of philosophy has the problem of knowledge stood so in the limelight; never before have such manifold and searching investigations, reaching out to include the very last details, been devoted to it. Yet it is highly questionable whether this vast extension of the problem has gone hand in hand with an equal profundity. For philosophy is gradually losing the leadership in this domain that it had held and treasured for centuries. The individual sciences will no longer delegate their authority but mean to see and judge for themselves.[2]
>
> . . . .
>
> The era of the great constructive programs, in which philosophy might hope to systematize and organize all knowledge, is past and gone. But the demand for synthesis and synopsis, for survey and comprehensive view, continues as before, and only by this sort of systematic review can a true historical understanding of the individual developments of knowledge be obtained.[3]

The study of knowledge is genuinely and primarily the philosophic task and it is of paramount importance in our time. Nothing could command our attention more, and we could do nothing more useful in this day of the atom bomb and

---

[2] Ernst Cassirer, *The Problem of Knowledge: Philosophy, Science and History since Hegel,* trans. William H. Woglom and Charles W. Hendel (New Haven, Conn.: Yale University Press, 1950), p. 10. Quoted by permission of the publisher.

[3] *Ibid.,* p. 19.

of universal unrest than to study knowledge. This seems to be a paradox, but the history of thought shows that most truth, especially the truth that is dynamic, is paradoxical.

In the quotation from Ernst Cassirer we meet with the statement that though now more than ever knowledge is being examined from every point of view, little permanent progress is being achieved. Let us indicate the truth behind this statement. In the days of Kant, Friedrich Schleiermacher was examining the structure of religious knowledge and took a point of view far beyond the rationalism which was typical of his time. He belonged to the age of Romanticism, and the Romantics were developing thought along the lines of the dictum of Pascal that the heart had its reasons which the head could never understand. While Hegel was developing a philosophy wherein thought and reality were made homogeneous so that the analysis of thought could show us the path of history, Sören Kierkegaard was appealing to the vision of the individual who saw reality in unique terms, found that reality was basically irrational, and laughed at rational categories. He used his own experience, his anguish and his fear, his loneliness and his frustration, to show that the Hegelian epistemology did not do justice to the problem of knowledge. The brilliant results of nineteenth-century science which brought forth the machine, the factory, the steamship, the locomotive, and in our century the automobile, the airplane, the radio, television, radar, and the release of atomic energy according to human design, all made an epistemology along empirical lines—every day better examined by men like Max Planck, Albert Einstein, Werner Heisenberg, Bertrand Russell—superb, simple, and unsatisfactory. Sigmund Freud showed that unconscious factors dominated thought and thinking. Karl Marx showed that society and economic conditions direct the thought of society's members. William James, Friedrich von Hügel, and Joseph Maréchal examined the mystic's experience in order to show unexpected capacities in thought. In other words, we now know that knowing is a very complex thing in which we can find simultaneously experience, sex, society, individual anguish, endocrine secretions, a God-seeking and a God-finding; we do not yet know what other elements may be found in it.

Besides alluding to all these factors that enter into knowledge, Cassirer pessimistically points out that no synthesis has been made. He, a philosopher, supposes that philosophy is not capable of the task.

The Notion of Metaphysics

The basic reason for this despair is the refusal to see in philosophy that which it is. It is a metaphysic. That word is so vague that we had better explain what we understand by it. On the supposition that the arithmetic which is commonly taught to our children in school is valid for measuring purposes on the earth on which we live, we can tell in advance that two million plus two million will make four million. There will be no need of any counting of apples or pigs or red corpuscles to come to this conclusion, and, as a matter of fact, when a blood count is done, no laboratory technician counts millions, though the report he makes will be in terms of millions. He uses ordinary arithmetic and comes to his final judgment. Now this faith in arithmetic is not empirical; it is not derived from the counting of millions. On our everyday plane of living we have never been deceived by arithmetic, and so it has a pragmatical confirmation, though no proof. The mind *sees* the truth of arithmetic. The logical positivists of the Vienna School do not like to call such things true, but the man in the street still clings to the notion that it is true that twenty-eight billion times two will be fifty-six billion, though it is humanly impossible to verify this proposition by experimental methods. When there is an appeal to the mind, without confirmation in experience, to the truth of a proposition, we are in metaphysics.

Each special science, e.g., physics, psychology, sociology, limits itself to an analysis of one area of our experience in

order to discern the particular set of relations existing in that
field and the generalizations which can be made about them.
Metaphysics, on the other hand, is the examination of the presuppositions of all our thinking. It is the study of the *a priori*
aspects of our knowledge and hence of the real, since knowledge
is the grasp of the real. Metaphysics, therefore, will reach beyond experience and beyond the research of any particular
science to study those primary aspects of reality which are imbedded in every object of experience and of scientific research
and without which these objects would not be intelligible.
Because it deals with the a priori its method cannot be empirical.

The philosophers of our day are very chary about metaphysics, though being philosophers they must be metaphysical.
The very logical positivists cannot prove by experience that
nothing is true that cannot be verified by experience. This is a
metaphysical stand in utter contradiction to metaphysics. Because of the modern philosophers' doubt as to the validity of
the primary philosophic task, they are in doubt as to their
capacity to give adequate answers to the epistemological problem. If the mind cannot solve this first problem posited by the
mind itself, how can it be good for giving any other answers?
This was the observation of Kant. If we are to examine knowledge from the philosophical point of view we must erect a
metaphysic of epistemology. That is the objective of the first
part of this study. There is no pretension of giving the last
answer or of setting down what has never been discovered before. It is only hoped that by the use of the philosophic method,
which is a metaphysical method, a deeper insight into the meaning of knowledge may be achieved.[4]

---

[4] The following are some authors who have worked along these lines. Gottlieb
Söhngen, *Sein und Gegenstand* (Münster, i.W.: Aschendorff, 1930). This work is
a reflection of a similar work of Nicolai Hartmann. Yves Simon, *Introduction à
l'ontologie du connaître* (Paris: Desclée, 1934). Fernand van Steenberghen,
Epistemology, trans. Martin J. Flynn (New York: Joseph F. Wagner, Inc., 1949).
Also useful is George van Riet, *L'Épistémologie Thomiste* (Ed. de l'Inst. sup. de
Phil., 1946).

2

The Phenomenology of Knowledge

Before we can make any reflection on an object we must first know the object. The phenomenologists are right when they insist that the first step in philosophy is an analysis of the phenomenon, which means an accurate description of the thing as that thing swims into our awareness. This must be met face to face before anything else can be done. This is no place to give definitions, because we have no right to define until the phenomenon has been completely surveyed. To begin with definitions is to expose the whole work to frustration or futility.

We are struck with one basic difficulty with an analysis of knowledge. The difficulty lies not in the doing but in the philosophical or logical right in essaying the task. An analysis of the phenomenon supposes that the mind (and by that we only mean the thinking or knowing process in man) can know, i.e., assimilate luminously the truth, at least the truth of thought or knowing. If we begin with this postulate, and without it we cannot begin, because truth is achieved only by knowledge or thought, then it seems that we have answered the problem of knowledge before we begin with it. The supposition of the investigation is that by thinking we can reach the truth about thought. If that is the supposition, then there is no problem of thought. We cannot simultaneously doubt it and use it to overcome doubt.

This difficulty was seen long ago. The reaction of the Thomist philosophers to the epistemological difficulties proposed by Kantianism, and by Cartesianism before it, was that all philosophy begins with the self-evident guarantee that thought is a means to truth. Hence there was for a time a refusal on the part of the Thomists to discuss the problem as a false one, just as the problem of what will happen when an irresistible force meets an immovable body is a false one. More recently Santayana dismissed the epistemological enquiry in much the same way by cavalierly appealing to what he calls an animal act of faith in knowledge which does not entertain serious doubts about knowledge itself.

However, Kant seemed to be the wiser. The fact of knowledge does raise questions about knowledge. These questions must be solved before any progress can be made in thought. As Kant clearly brought out, however, there can be no question whether or not knowledge or thinking *is*. That is an unescapable datum which founds the philosophic enterprise. "That I do know" is given. "That I can know" is a conclusion. "What is this knowledge that I have" and "what does it give me" are problems that need to be solved. Hence we follow the phenomenological procedure; we shall examine knowledge as given and examine it with our only instrument, knowledge.

The Forms of Knowledge as Given

It is not our ambition to discover all the forms of knowledge. Suffice it for our purpose that we analyze phenomenologically the more recognized forms of knowledge or thinking: awareness or pure consciousness, empirical perception through categories, metaphysical intuition, reason, faith, and mystical experience. It would be a mistake to think that, since these are distinct forms of knowledge, they therefore occur in isolation from one another in the actual stream of our thought. At one and the same moment you may perceive a person, place him in several universal categories, e.g., tall, handsome, friend, reason about him from his behavior, and be conscious of the acts of perceiving him, reasoning about him, and experiencing the feelings and emotions that may accompany the presence of a friend; however, although these forms of knowledge are not separate in our experience, they are distinct, for, as we shall see, each is a capacity for presenting to us a different content. It is only by treating each capacity and its object separately that we shall be able to understand the precise functioning of each in the complex unity of the act of knowing.

Awareness or pure consciousness

All will admit that this is the basic form of knowledge. All knowledge is awareness, but there is a *pure awareness* which we call consciousness. I not only know things but knowledge itself is known. Consciousness cannot be defined, because it is the original datum. We can point to it and let the hearer recognize it in his experience. To help to that end we can call consciousness the assimilation, the registering, the absorption of luminous content, but this is hardly a definition. It is simply a stimulating description which appeals to a metaphor derived from our eye's reaction to light.

Phenomenologically, consciousness does not entail a substantial, perduring self, the source of action. It can be called "I," but this is only shorthand. The "I" is the complex of activity that is registered. Phenomenologically it has no other meaning.

Consciousness, therefore, is the awareness of "I" states. Such states may be cognitive, e.g., I am aware of seeing something colored or of hearing a sound, or of grasping a universal meaning such as "justice"; they may be affective, as when I am aware of an emotional state such as being happy or sad; they may be conative, as when I am aware of desiring refreshment and of willing to obtain it. Consciousness never reaches *otherness* directly; it can reach it only as a content of the "I," and it can make no affirmation as to its validity. In fact, consciousness of itself never affirms. It does not even picture or represent. It merely "sees." It does not deal with the past nor with the future. It does not deal with anything that is not existentially in act. The terms direct and indirect consciousness are misnomers. There can be no consciousness which is not altogether direct. The so-called indirect consciousness is reason working on the data of consciousness, or better, of memory, which seems to be a process working on consciousness in cold storage.

Consciousness is the basis of all knowledge. That there can be no unconscious knowledge is readily admitted. The Freudian unconscious ideas are not knowledge but determined urges to action which can be expressed by ideas. The Freudian "unconscious" does not "know" what it wants. It is structural dynamism.

Empirical perception through categories

Although consciousness is the basis of knowledge, neither is its content rich nor would man go far in knowledge by it alone. Only a god could know otherness by consciousness because the "I" would be given as model and source of the other. Most of our knowledge is referred to the other and not to the "I," even though through the "I" the other is attained. The other is categorized content of consciousness, which is the carrier of all knowledge. Phenomenologically we cannot say how the other enters into consciousness, though we generally call the process sensation and have imaged a psychological process whereby this is supposed to be done. The difficulty with this whole image is that it introduces those terrible phrases, "inside the mind" and "outside the mind," into epistemological discussions, which phrases already commit us to a metaphysic not dictated by the phenomenon itself.

All that the phenomenon says is that we have achieved as a content of consciousness a perception of an existing other, rendered meaningful by categories or concepts. On the examination of the phenomenon of this kind of knowledge we simply can state no more.

It is clear that we must admit different kinds of such perception. Central sense[1] or *sensus communis* perceives for categorization present "I" states. Memory perceives past conscious awareness and expresses it by categories. The mechanism of this kind of perception is incapable of an image, for images demand stability in space; but memory, as Bergson insisted, goes into time, which is a coordinate factor that will not be properly depicted by a timeless line as would be required by an image.[2] The perception of a cat or a dog as a content of consciousness permits a mechanical picture of process, though no such process has yet been satisfactory. The reason for this is that consciousness is not image, and all images are dimensional. This means a limit which consciousness readily transcends. It was the weakness of the mechanical materialism of the last century that tried to reduce all knowledge to an image. That type of thinking is not praised in our time.

Let it be remembered that the phenomenon of empirical perception through categories does not betray the psychological process involved. The depiction of such a process is only a rationalization. The whole concept of sensation needs serious rethinking because of this fact. Kant was not far from true appreciation of epistemological truth when he reduced sensation to the acquisition of empirical data which would not be true

---

[1] By central sense we mean the capacity of the mind to synthesize the varied data of the several senses into an organized pattern. For example, in perceiving an apple, the red color, the smooth texture, the slight odor, the sweet taste, although perceived by separate senses, are attributed to one object of our consciousness.

[2] Henri Bergson, *Matter and Memory*, trans. N. M. Paul and W. S. Palmer (New York: The Macmillan Company, 1950), especially Chap. III, and *Time and Free Will*, trans. F. L. Pogson (London: George Allen & Unwin, Ltd., 1950), pp. 99-104 and 181-182.

human knowledge until it had taken on the forms of the categories. In this sense his famous axiom: perception without concepts is blind and concepts without perception are empty.

However, psychology and physiology have given us much to think about in the matter of the corporal factor in empirical knowledge. No one today would reduce the senses to five. No one believes that they deal only with extra-subjective reality. Only God knows how many there are, and Dr. Rhine of Duke University has opened wide the field to the existence of "senses" whose function and physical constitution are completely mysterious.[3] We know from Freud that the unconscious makes us not quite objective in perception, if that word can have any meaning whatever in today's knowledge. Narcotics can influence the sensational apparatus. Endocrine action modifies sense perception. Fatigue will do it. That there is a bodily function in empirical perception seems quite beyond discussion, and the neurologists have done interesting experiments, the results of which are not so clear. Just what a vision center in the brain is, or whether the brain acts by parts or as a whole, is still vague. Many of the questions that were formerly discussed, for example—if it is the eye that sees—are today meaningless. Man in the use of the whole optic apparatus —eye, nerves, and brain—sees.

One result of all this investigation is to put no extra-personal objectivity in the image that accompanies knowledge of the other, though it is certainly the most vivid element in the consciousness of the empirical perception. The new physics has reduced the material world to a stretch of energy which cannot be imaged. What a rose is like is something a physicist can understand and express in mathematical equations. He has simply thrown away any hope of "imaging" it, and the image that accompanies his knowledge he simply ignores. In the light of these findings, it is rather obscurantist to ask if the sense im-

---

[3] J. B. Rhine, *New Frontiers of the Mind* (New York: Farrar & Rhinehart, Inc., 1937) and *The Reach of the Mind* (New York: William Sloane Associates, 1947).

age is objectively representative. The whole basis of modern science both in physics and chemistry is that the sense image has nothing to tell us about the object except to indicate that it is there and related to the image as a whole and in parts.

This type of thinking is not at all foreign to Thomism, for Thomas always insisted that truth was formally in intellection and not in sensation. Sensation can be said to be cognitive only insofar as it is an element in cognition which in its true stage, i.e., the stage where truth must be discovered, can only be found in intellectual assent.[4]

What is basic here is that empirical knowledge by categories is essentially different from consciousness which is pure awareness without categories. Both may be called empirical because they entail experience, but they are different in their reaction to the experimented. Both are intellectual, but in empirical knowledge a process is entailed which must include the material aspect of man. A pure spirit could not achieve knowledge by empirical discovery.

The other element that is important here is that *existence* of otherness is given by empirical knowledge. Except through empirical knowledge we cannot know the otherly existence. Consciousness cannot give it. Concerning mysticism we shall speak later.

Metaphysical intuition

In the preceding process of knowledge we saw that empirical perception of the other entails categorization. Here we promptly meet with difficulty. By what right does the thinking process categorize? Independently of experience, though not without it, a mind can perceive categories, not as existing things, but as realities. We can conceive the category of mountains of green cheese, though as far as we know none exists.

---

[4] Cf. Rudolph Allers, "Intellectual Cognition," in *Essays in Thomism,* ed. R. E. Brennan (New York: Sheed & Ward Inc., 1942), pp. 41ff.

We can discuss future generations of men, though they do not exist.

As we have seen above, Plato and Aristotle wrestled with this problem openly. The Middle Ages, before Thomas, did so openly, and the post-Thomistic scholastics rejected Thomas for a pure nominalism, which is the solution of all thoroughgoing empiricists. It was the question of the universals.

To students brought up exclusively on the scholasticism current until a few years ago, it seems silly to enter into this phase of knowledge. They thought they had solved it with the Aristotelian empirical solution. However, the question comes up again today and an examination of the phenomenon of knowledge has led the phenomenologists to re-examine the whole question.

The problem as it stands today is whether categorization, or in the older language, the knowledge of the universal, is a different kind of knowledge from the knowledge of the other as existent, and from consciousness. Plato thought that it was and gave a metaphysical solution to the problem. He believed that the mind had immediate contact with a whole plane of reality which is the reality of the category. According to him by a fanciful myth that he used, the mind had a reminiscence of this reality which it had directly intuited *en topo noeto*[5] before its present condition. This is a myth and we must not take the myth literally, as Plato certainly would not have us do so. To-day we would say that the mind directly intuits categories of being and places the empirical in the category that corresponds to it. The phenomenologists call it the intuition of meaning. Augustine spoke of it as an intuition of the divine Ideas. This solution is strictly *metaphysical,* as it puts into reality the category. The solution of the problem is in terms of *being.*

Aristotle, a materialist at heart, refused to recognize a reality

---

[5] Literally this means "in the mind place." This is to indicate that the mind is its categorizing function grasps realities distinct from the sensible realities of the material world which it grasps in empirical perception.

of the category beyond the reality of the things categorized. For Plato, the categorizing principle, the model and exemplar, the Idea, was beyond the things exemplified. Aristotle took this external principle and put it into things. Everything had its categorizing principle within itself and the mind simply recognized it in the empirical grasp of the existing other. Aristotle worked out the psychological process which is called abstraction. It must be borne in mind that the abstraction theory is not a metaphysical theory but a *psychological* one, though it does suppose a metaphysic for the real. Aristotle did not proceed metaphysically in the question of knowledge.

Thomas followed both Aristotle and Plato. This is the paradox of Thomism, and also its greatness. Aquinas was too much imbued with his reading of Aristotle not to take over his theory of abstraction, but he was also too much influenced by Augustine to drop out his Ideas. Hence Thomas holds for a double principle of categorization. The proximate one is the empirical other, and the remote one, the divine Idea, is beyond it. There is no difficulty in doing what Thomas did, for as we have said, Aristotle's abstraction myth is only a psychological apparatus and not a metaphysical analysis of knowledge. As Thomas says in the question of the divine Ideas,[6] there must be divine Ideas, for otherwise it would be impossible to have reality that falls into categories. In the same question he denies that he is Platonic, because his categories are *not existent empirical* realities—which was never in the mind of Plato, but of which Aristotle charged him.

After Thomas, categorization was either a psychological structure of the mind, as Kant wished it, or a mere human device to gather together empirical existents into economical groups, as the positivists wished it.

Before we give allegiance to any school, let us analyze the phenomenon of the category or universal concept.

(1) It is clear that before an object can be rendered mean-

---

[6] St. Thomas Aquinas, *Summa Theologica*, I, q. 15, 1; cf. I, 84, 5.

ingful by category, the category must be known. Such priority may be merely logical, but the priority is there. Before I can declare a thing to be white, I must know what whiteness is, for otherwise I cannot call anything white. To use a distinction of Aristotelian logic, it is not necessary that such a concept be distinct. It suffices that the concept be clear.

(2) It is also clear that the concept of categorical whiteness cannot be verified in a singular object, because whiteness is a class concept and not an individual trait.

(3) However, a class concept can be referred to individuals of the class, otherwise it would not be a class concept, which supposes members.

(4) A class concept is not the same as a group or collectivity concept, because a group or collectivity is always conceived as singular, and capable of existence as such.

It seems just to agree with Kant that such a class concept cannot be derived from the empirical other, because this is always individual by the law of existence. When this is said, we are rejecting the Aristotelian abstraction theory as a metaphysical explanation, though such a rejection does not imply a rejection of the myth as a psychological explanation.

It seems just to agree with the phenomenologists that Kant is not true to the phenomenon of knowledge in supposing that the concept derives from the structural dynamism of knowledge. The class notion is content and not merely form.

The final conclusion is that we must admit in knowledge a form that intuits classes. This in Platonic mythology is the reminiscence of the Idea. In phenomenology this is called the intuition of meanings. In Bergson, followed by Paul Foulquié, S.J., this is the metaphysical intuition. In Santayana it is the intuition of essences. By recent Thomists it is called intuitive abstraction, where the Platonic element of Thomas is kept and the psychological apparatus of Thomistic Aristotelianism is also preserved.

A negative conclusion is that we must drop once and for all

the nominalist deduction of the universals, which was so common among scholastics of recent times. According to this explanation, the mind compares different individuals and recognizes similarity, and thus produces a class concept. The difficulty in this explanation is that it is not true to the phenomenon of knowledge. Similarity means the sharing of a common characteristic. Hence for the mind to recognize similarity, it must have already seen in its object a class characteristic, which is the universal or class concept. Hence there can be no appeal to similarity as the source of the class concept, because similarity already supposes the presence of the class concept. To recognize similarity, it is necessary to have recognized in the similar objects a common note, which is the universal class concept.

Nor can we accept the old materialist supposition that a class is a vague individual which will serve as a diagrammatic representation or symbol for many individuals. The class is the clearest thing we have. There is nothing vague about it.

Hence we must give a fuller meaning to the old distinction of the direct and reflex universal. It is not valid to say that the direct universal precedes the indirect or reflex universal metaphysically. It can readily be admitted that it precedes psychologically, and that is the only meaning for the axiom *nihil in intellectu quod non prius in sensu.*[7] Metaphysically prior to the direct universal there is a clear but not distinct conception of the class or universal. Reflection makes this clear conception distinct. The direct universal is only the universal giving meaning to a concrete individual, for without the class reference, the concrete empirical is meaningless. It is a functional use of the universal. The reflex universal is pure intellection rendered distinct by reflection, that is, by turning back on a previously known object.

One last conclusion from phenomenology is that the human mind is intuitive. It can see certain reality in itself, even though that reality is other. However, such intuition is not of existents

---

[7] There is nothing in the intellect which was not previously in the senses.

but of class categories. Hence the mind is endowed with a double intuition. First of all, it has an intuition of its own activity without concepts. Secondly, through concepts it has an intuition of the class, or the abstract, or the universal. The concept is the expression of this intuition and for the psychological process in which it is realized, according to the recent Thomist phrase, intuitive abstraction is a very just label.[8]

Reason

By reason we mean the capacity to achieve fuller truth from truth already acquired through intuition and empirical perception. Reasoning is not truly discovering, for it works on previous discoveries and by concentration derives the full commitment of previous knowledge. Reason can never discover either existents or even essentials, but can only manifest that such existents or essentials are implicated in a given thought.

Aristotle in his logic showed admirably how reason works, for he identified it with the psychological process called the demonstrative syllogism. That logic has not been transcended by the work done by the modern logicians. They have only amplified what he had to say. For reasons of simplicity Aristotle dealt only with the simple proposition. In his syllogism he will not permit compound propositions. However, the mathematicians deal with the compound proposition and they have extended the field of logic. Yet they insist, with right, that they are not putting up a rival system to that of Aristotle. They are merely assailing the task that he refused to handle. As propositions become more complex, and as the mind cannot keep all the elements simultaneously in attention, the modern logicians, taking their cue from arithmetic, use symbols for different combinations, so that it will not be necessary to keep all the elements in mind. Logic has advanced but it has not been revolutionized.

---

[8] Cf. A. J. McNicholl, O.P., "Physical Metaphysics," *The Thomist,* XII (October 1949), pp. 438-439.

The process of reasoning has been known ever since Aristotle produced the *Organun*. A class concept or universal is analyzed, and the elements true of it are all true of the member of the class. In negative fashion, a note rejected by the class concept is rejected by every member of the class. The validity of this process is evident in terms of the meaning of class concept and member of that class. The mind spontaneously goes through this process by the dynamism of class concept categorization, and this is the only way in which the mind perceives otherness, or even "I" states as presented by sensation.

The metaphysical validity of such action derives from metaphysical intuition. Empirically we cannot prove the validity of the conclusion of a syllogism. Though experience may in sensible knowledge confirm the conclusion by experimental verification in this or that case, or in a number of cases, the truth of the conclusion is general and experience gives us only the individual. This brings up the whole notion of proof. In Aristotelian philosophy proof is always reasoned conclusion. The scholastics saw a flaw in this principle with their maxim: *contra factum non valet illatio*,[9] which is more than a debater's instrument. Descartes in his methodology wished to make all proof rational. The empiricists, and especially the scientists of today, do not understand proof in this way. For them proof is always experimental verification, and where such is not forthcoming or is impossible, there is no proof. Where empirical verification is by definition impossible, scientists declare the proposition to be meaningless. Where empirical verification is not impossible, but not yet achieved, the proposition is hypothetical.

Between the old "rationalism" and the new "empiricism" a new position has arisen. It is called intellectualism.[10] This theory supposes with the empiricists that proof is possible without

---

[9] Inference must yield in the face of the facts.

[10] Cf. Pierre Rousselot, S.J., *The Intellectualism of St. Thomas*, trans. J. E. O'Mahoney (New York: Sheed & Ward Inc., 1935).

mere rationalistic proof by analysis. It makes much of the principle, *contra factum non valet illatio,* and it seeks for consistency as a sign of proof, where consistency takes into account all the factors manifested by knowledge on every level. Against the empiricists and with the rationalists, it supposes that proof is possible by the mere use of thought already acquired and also gives to pure rationalism a place in the formation of proof. In fact, today the battle is not between rationalism and empiricism, between coherence with experience and deduction from a closed determined compound proposition, but between intellectualism and empiricism, between consistency of thought on the whole plane of thinking and the restriction of thought to the empirical plane.

One more element that has entered into the study of rational thinking is a distinction that must be made between pure analysis and true syllogistic procedure. To say that, since man is a rational animal, it follows that man is corporeal, is not a true ratiocination. The syllogism that expresses this final proposition is only a pedagogic device and not a true syllogism. Animality means corporeity. Nothing new has been brought forth. The implicit has only been made explicit. To be a true syllogism it is necessary that the minor proposition be true by experience, or by another intuition. Thus because John is a man, evident by experience, it follows that John is corporeal, for that is an element in the class concept "man." Pure analysis is not rationalism but intellectualism, based on metaphysical intuition. Reasoning always supposes some element of experience, or other intuition, made more luminous by analysis of a prior class concept.

Now it is true that all classes of positivism must reject this explanation of the dynamism of the syllogism or ratiocination. In strict theory, though not in practice, they do not suppose the conclusion to be true unless it is verified experimentally. It is only hypothesis until that moment arrives, and every man is free to speculate by any principle that he wishes. The so-called laws of thought are not laws at all but convenient rules which may be changed if they lead to experimental verification. The conceptual dynamism is not definitive and is accepted as a cultural inheritance. The positivists will not even admit with Kant that it is a psychological structure. Hence they experiment with the elimination of all laws of thought; the principle of the excluded middle is not considered basic, and there have been attempts made to drop the principle of contradiction or reduce it to linguistic law.

As we shall see later in dealing with scientific methodology, there is here a complete relegation of conceptual dynamism. The out-and-out positivist simply denies that it exists. He admits that he uses concepts in coming to conclusions, but this is not necessary and no value can be given to the conclusion a priori, i.e., before experimental verification. However, on the analysis of the phenomenon of knowledge, such a procedure seems utterly arbitrary and really frustrating. Reason certainly enters into science, as all sciences readily and proudly admit. It cannot work except by certain principles and laws. These principles and laws flow from the analysis of certain basic concepts, as Kant's derivation of the principles of the understanding showed. The scientist is committed to the postulate that conceptual analysis is valid, even though he may question the validity of this or that conceptual analysis. All logic is based on this supposition and logic is the way science proceeds. Today its prime method of procedure is the pure logic of mathematics.

Faith

In knowledge we are aware that certain thoughts are justified to the knowing mind by the observation that someone said that it is true. In this type of knowledge the mind has no intuition of the object, has no personal experience of the object nor does it reason to the object. There is a mediate experience. Someone has experienced the object and communicates to us his experience and we thus share it, and like the direct experimenter we know it. This kind of knowledge is a cultural phenomenon and postulates a social union of human beings.

Faith is the form of knowledge that is quantitatively the most prevalent in the total output of knowledge of the other. Our parentage, the activities of other men, and distant nature, the state of the earth in far-off places, the past, the experimental sources of so many scientific conclusions, the inner states of our companions, are all known to us by faith.

This form of knowledge, so all-pervading as it is, clearly brings with it a peril that is always felt by the knower. In this field perhaps more than in any other do we realize that we are exposed to error, that state of thought when we have categorized an existent or supposed existent falsely. Nevertheless, we feel justified in relying on this type of knowledge in spite of the fact that it has so often misled us.

Religious faith is of this kind, if faith is used as a form of knowledge and not as a form of confidence as it usually is by non-Catholics. The Catholic notion of faith adheres strictly to this type of knowledge and Catholic theology insists that supernatural faith is knowledge, for it is an intellectual act; however, there is a double difference. First of all, the other person, because of whom we believe in the Catholic theory of supernatural faith, is God, the personal source of all things, who is supposed to have communicated His knowledge. Secondly, there is a supernatural modification of the thinking apparatus so that it can rise to a higher level of knowledge. This kind of faith must be studied in theology and not in philosophy.

Mystical experience

In the last sixty years much attention has been paid to the phenomenon of mysticism. As far as our question is concerned, we can limit ourselves to the definition of mysticism whereby it is an intuition of the Absolute without categories. It is to be noted that it is like consciousness which perceives the existent "I", but different because this perceives an other. It is like the empirical grasp of the other in what we call sensible knowledge, but here there are no categories and there is no sensitive collaboration in the knowledge itself. It is like the intuition of meanings, but here it is not an inexistent that is perceived, but the prime existent.

The discussion on this point is too great for us to commit ourselves.[11] All that we can say is that if there is such a phenomenon, and the analysis of a large and constant tradition of cases seems to warrant the truth of the supposition, then there is in man a capacity for intuition of not only "I" states and inexistent essences or meanings, but also of the prime other in which all others are imbedded. We can say no more about it, because in the usual phenomenon of knowledge this type of thought is not given. Hence we must leave it as an open question. However, this kind of knowledge undoubtedly expands the knowing possibilities of man beyond his expectations.

General Conclusions

As a consequence of the analysis of the phenomenon of knowledge given above we may now set down some conclusions.

(1) There are at least five levels of knowledge, pure consciousness, empirical perception through categories, metaphysical intuition, reason, and faith.

(2) All knowledge is based primarily on intuition, though it begins in time with empirical contact. The general condition of all knowledge is the intuition of "I" states of which categorized knowledge is one. Furthermore, all empirical knowledge recognized in terms of categories supposes an intuition of essences or meanings.

(3) The perfect form of empirical knowledge through cate-

---

[11] Cf. Joseph Maréchal, S.J., *Studies in the Psychology of the Mystics*, trans. Algar Thorold (London: Burns, Oates & Washbourne, Ltd., 1927).

gories is expressed in the judgment where the object indicated receives its meaning in the predicate of judicial affirmation.

(4) The dynamism of the judgment is the copula which at least by implication is always "is." Hence the first categorical intuition about an object is its "isness."

(5) The copula "is" does not always mean exactly the same thing. It may be the *is* of being non-existent, e.g., a man is a rational animal, in which we are affirming the *isness* of essence; and it may be the *is* of existence rendered luminous by the *isness* of essence in the predicate, e.g., John is young. Here there is a double intuition.

(6) *Is* is incapable of definition. Its meaning is without category, and all who use judgments understand it. Though it cannot be defined, it can be contemplated and studied, making ontology possible.

(7) Where knowledge works without categories as in consciousness and mysticism, there can be no communication of the content knowledge except as a felt state, because communication is through categories. Hence the complete conscious subject is always incommunicable, and he is always closed off from all other reals except from the non-intuited prime real in which all others are imbedded. This accounts for the solitude and pain of which the existentialists speak. Hence the mystic's vision is also incommunicable, because categories must be used in communication, and yet the knowledge achieved was without categories.

(8) Empirical knowledge, which is a fusion of experimentally given data with intuited categories, is an inferior kind of knowledge, but is yet the only kind at our normal disposal for knowing existing other objects. It is inferior because it does not grasp the object in itself but must render it luminous by reference to a class meaning.

(9) Reasoning, whether the strict ratiocination of the true syllogism, or the apparent reasoning of sheer meaning-analysis,

is always imperfection, because the content of the reasoning was not seen simultaneously with the meaning, which had to be the object of reflection and analysis.

(10) Reasoning, though as much a form of knowledge as any other, is inferior to and not superior to the other forms of knowledge. It has no superiority or primacy. It is therefore erroneous to identify intelligence, the faculty of knowing, with reason.

(11) Reason cannot make prime discoveries, because it is an analysis of already achieved meanings or class concepts.

(12) Reason has a veto power. Nothing can go counter to reason, because reason declares certain combinations of meanings and objects as meaningless, essenceless, but essences are given in all existence but one.

(13) The denial of the validity of any of the five forms of knowledge is a sign of faulty analysis of the phenomenon of knowledge. Though the average man does not seem able to affirm the mystical form of knowledge, this gives him no right to deny it.

(14) To the age-old question, is the object inside or outside the mind, we must answer that under these terms the question is meaningless. Inside and outside are spatial objects which are content of knowledge and not backgrounds for the phenomenon. The nature of the "I" is not given in awareness so as to act as the reference point of in and out. Yet the words "extra-mental" and "objective" are innocent in intention. They are merely post-epistemological labels prematurely dragged into epistemology. Truth is the knowing or intentional grasp of the real. Toward it we are driven and this drive is intuited in the knowing act. Knowledge is true when it has achieved the real. That knowledge does achieve the real is given in knowledge, because the copula of judgment is "is," the verbal expression for reality. Except for the intuition of reality as given by judicial affirmation in terms of the copula "is," we have no

other way of achieving the meaning of reality. Hence, since the content of knowledge is given under the wings of "is," given knowledge, it is likewise given that we reach the real, and thus truth. The epistemological problem is solved. It is not an a priori question to be answered, but a commitment involved in the analysis of knowledge. The question is only rhetorical; it is not ontological.

As a result of this observation we can criticize certain epistemological stands known in history.

(a) All philosophical empiricism, i.e., the metaphysical stand that only the empirical grasp of the existent other is possible, simply refuses to accept the sum total of knowledge and even refuses to recognize the category-reality implied in the empirical enterprise. With this rejection, sensism, positivism of the Spencer-Comte variety, or the newest form of logical positivism, fall.

(b) Materialism and idealism are not epistemological questions. They are conclusions of the analysis of being, which is ontology. Both forms of philosophy simply suppose that being is univocally homogeneous. The materialist, because he accepts the findings of empirical grasping of other existents, supposes therefore that all being is of the same constitution as the objects that evoke knowledge by bulk impact. The idealist, because he recognizes the reality of thought, supposes that all reality is of the same texture. The phenomenon of knowledge, however, does not warrant such an affirmation of the univocal homogeneity of being.

(c) Kant's position was suicidal. He set up from the beginning two objects as the norm of truth—one unintelligible and the other intelligible. It is perfectly clear that the unintelligible is the same as nothing. Nothing can be said about it; it cannot be conceived; it has no face, figure, or comprehensibility. To drag it into a discussion is the same as lifting one's self by one's boot straps. The unintelligible has no place in philosophy and it cannot be a pole in dialectical discourse. Unintelligible and unreal are synonyms, and consequently the unintelligible must be dropped from all consideration whether in life or in thought.

(d) The extreme existentialism of the Jean-Paul Sartre type is simply a refusal to analyze the phenomenon of thought and that is why the more genuine forms of existentialism, as proposed by Heidegger and Jaspers, refuse to recognize Sartre as legitimate. Not only is existence given in knowledge, but also essence, through the identical copula "is."

(e) The stand of George Santayana is not adequate. He admits the reality of essences and admits that we intuit them. He merely restricts the term of knowledge to empirical grasp of the existent. This is arbitrary. Knowledge gives him no such grounds for distinction. His so-called materialism is really pure skepticism as to the possibility of knowing certainly the existent except by pleasing speculations. In contradiction to his own teaching he limits reality to existence, which he denies is definitively knowable. Yet Santayana is very near to the solution of the epistemological question which he pretends to dismiss as useless.

(f) The phenomenologists have done justice to the epistemological question, but it is not so clear that they have established a valid metaphysic. They fall inevitably into either logical positivism or idealism.

(g) William James with his pragmatism, or John Dewey with his instrumentalism, do not approach the problem rightly. It is not because they say that truth is the useful, for they do not say this, but rather because they are skeptical as to the possibility of truth, and therefore seek for utility in their investigations rather than truth; however, this is fallacious because impossible. The problem immediately arises: what is the truly useful? And there is truth right back with us. The Dewey answer, namely, that is useful which works, is no answer because

Nazi-ism and communism both work. Ultimately by "work-ing" they mean the actualization of someone's desires. This is the most hopeless of all norms. Philosophy does not teach me how to realize desire, but to discipline desire to reality.

3

The Problem
of Certitude

As a result of our analysis of the phenomenon of knowledge we have rejected the question, "can the mind achieve objective truth?", as illegitimate. We have stated on the grounds of analysis of the phenomenon in the light of the metaphysic there contained, that my knowledge on any level gives me the real. To grasp the real is to have the truth, for truth can have no other meaning. Having rejected a false epistemological problem we must essay the true one.

What is the true one? It is this, "How is error possible and what steps can we take to avoid it?" It cannot be "is error necessary and unavoidable?" because this would be saying that we cannot reach truth by knowledge, which denies what we have said in the conclusion of the analysis of the phenomenon of knowledge. That error has existed and does exist is a patent fact in history. Someone has said that it is too hard to teach beginners, not because they know nothing, but because they know so many things that "ain't so." Most learning consists in unlearning. How then can error be avoided?

First, intuition can never be wrong. It simply sees, and it can be no more wrong than a mirror can be wrong in reflecting a face. Hence consciousness can never be wrong, but as it affirms nothing, there is no danger of it being questioned. Hence also the essences given by intuition are always validly given. How-

ever, in the judgment of empirical grasp of the existent other
through categories, a false category may have been placed on
the object which is never seen in itself. Thus too, a witness
can lead us astray and often does. The third observer has con-
founded essences in his categorization of the event. Reason,
also, can be wrong, because the rules of logic have not been followed, and a fallacy has slipped in, or in reasoning in its widest
sense, an exact analysis was not made of an essence, or one essence has been unobservedly substituted for the one under contemplation.

In other words, we have restricted error to the field of
empirical observation and reasoning. Now for empirical observation the danger of error is so great that Plato thought that
in this form of knowledge we never reach certitude, i.e., secure
assent. Santayana had an idea quite akin to this. However,
these stands seem to be too skeptical. Empirical grasp seems
to be generally valid with reference to the wider categories under which the other has been achieved. This is especially true
with reference to the judgment that I see such a thing. That
I see cannot be questioned. Whether the thing seen is actually
such, or truly so, can at times be doubted. Likewise, the common element in a long series of experimental knowledge, especially when it is confirmed by the testimony of others, is valid,
for otherwise empirical grasp would not give us the real at
all, which it does by anterior commitment. It cannot always
be wrong, for then it would not be a source of knowledge.
These common elements will usually be the more generic
attributes of the existent other. For the more specific determi-
nations of the empirical object, especially the data achieved
by minute scientific investigation, there is hardly the same
guarantee that we have reached the empirical object with all
the security which is possible where intuition is had. There is
always a blind spot in the cognition of the empirical other. The
Thomists have noted this blind spot in the assertion that the
individual is never known in his individual being, i.e., known

as an individual essence. This does not mean that we do not know the individual. We do, and we know him more vividly than we know the class notion. However, it can be known only in terms of the universal, never in terms of the individual. The Suarezian theory that the individual is known before the universal is only true in the sense that before any kind of knowledge is possible concerning an individual (and with the individual knowledge begins), contact is needed with that individual and the first act of knowledge deals with the individual. However, as an individual he is met, but not conceived.

This brings up the question of certitude, or rather this whole question is the same as the problem of certitude. Certitude may be defined as the security and tranquillity of assent. There is a distinction made between subjective and objective certitude. In subjective certitude the security and tranquillity *de facto* are there. In objective certitude they are there *de jure*. The epithets subjective and objective are hardly apt. It would be better to speak of unwarranted and warranted certitude.

Certitude and Truth

The relationship of certitude to truth is patent. The reason why a doubt, i.e., insecurity in assent, arises is because the real has not imposed itself on the knower. When the real has been grasped despotically, the subject has no doubts. He will never doubt that he feels pain, though he can be made to doubt that there is a physical source of such pain. He will never doubt that being and non-being cannot be affirmed of the same subject. In such knowledge the real has been assimilated in itself. Doubt only arrives when the real is met blindly and rendered luminous by reference to something else. However, the leap is made spontaneously and necessarily and is thus a natural leap and carries with it the guarantee of nature. If the leap is made according to the instincts of the faculty employed by the knower in his search for the real, he feels quite secure. If we are engaged in conversation with several persons, we do not doubt that those persons are there, though we readily admit that we can be mistaken in this matter, but the possibility does not move us to doubt. Just as the driver of the auto feels quite at ease when he presses the proper buttons and pulls the proper levers, so the thinker acting in accord with the process of knowledge, is at ease.

Nothing was more profound than the insight of the scholastics who distinguished between three levels of certitude. They spoke of metaphysical certitude, the certitude achieved in the knowledge of conscious intuition and the objects of metaphysical intuition. In this kind of knowledge the object is given in itself. Nothing is given, or the object is given; hence when given, perfect knowledge is achieved. There is no room for doubt. The awareness is pellucid from the beginning and adhesion is despotically extracted.

In physical certitude the situation is different. The physical is the existent, and the existent must be met in experience and rendered luminous by reference to the metaphysical. The object is never seen in itself, and hence the ease and tranquillity of metaphysical knowledge is absent. Yet since empirical knowledge is knowledge, there is no doubt in principle. There can only be doubt as to the true use of the experimental apparatus, and unless the knower is moved by some positive sign of misuse of his knowing instruments, he will not be ill at ease.

In moral certitude, where ease is felt in accepting a reality on faith, we are met with new difficulties. Not only can there be malfunction of the physical apparatus of empirical perception, but the personal element of the communicant makes us pause. We can never enter into the consciousness of another, and consequently we do not know the whys and wherefores of his action. He may be maliciously or pathologically intent on deceiving us. Yet again, unless we are confronted by some particular manifestation of such intent, we are not disturbed because of the general possibility, and we take his word serenely.

It is quite clear that the certitude achieved on these three distinct levels is not the same. No true motive for insecurity ever pops up on the metaphysical level. There, only the epistemological question can arise, and that question, as we have said, is rhetorical and not real. On the other two levels, where the object is not met in itself, there is only a presumption in favor of assent. Since knowledge is given on this level and since knowledge is a structural dynamism, we accept the assent on the presumption that we are moving in accord with our dynamism. The presumption gives way to fact, and the assent is always reformable. It is here that the animal faith of Santayana works. In terms of the action that is required because we live, we give the assent, and we are humanly justified in doing so. Justified assent is the measure of certitude on the physical and moral levels. The certitude is prudential. It cannot be more.

Motive of Certitude

This brings up the Cartesian question of the motive of certitude. In his *Discourse on Method* Descartes makes clear and distinct conception the motive for secure assent. By clear and distinct conception he means the grasp of content in knowledge in such a way that the mind cannot refuse assent, but the assent is despotically extracted. Clear and distinct for him are the same as the undeniable. This he called evidence, and Cartesian evidence has subsequently been called subjective evidence, because the knowing subject's incapacity to deny is the mark of clarity. Now, what Descartes called evidence fell on the level of intuition. That the intuited is evident is a truism. Hence there is no quarrel with him on his doctrine of evidence. We must quarrel with him in his attempt to reduce all certitude to one kind. We will not, and cannot, make the assent on all levels of knowledge the assent due to intuition. His attempt to draw all knowledge from the intuited failed and he plunged philosophy into a paralysis of rationalism. Prudential certitude as achieved on other levels is a true certitude but of a different order. This certitude makes science and history possible, and it must not be considered as a poor relation. Even if it had no such high contribution to make in the field of thought, it would still be noble, because it is the kind of certitude that we need for action. Act we must because we are existent human beings. Even a refusal to act is action, for it is a choice. All such action must be justified prudentially. Since act I must, I can certainly follow my spontaneous dynamism if no moving warning is presented to the contrary. To abstain from all assent except where the assent is that of metaphysical intuition simply means that I shall die, and the instinct for life moves me as despotically as the instinct to assent to the metaphysically intuited. It is prudent to obey this instinct as long as there is no positive good to be attained by not doing so. The mere avoidance of error on the empirical level is no such positive good. Many such errors are quite indifferent. Whether the sun goes around the earth or the earth around the sun is a matter which is indifferent to the work of the ship's navigator. Any error he may have is not pertinent to the life of action.

Jaime Balmes in his *Criterio* developed the notion of evidence as presented by Descartes and evolved what was subsequently known in scholastic circles as the doctrine of objective evidence. William James made fun of the notion, but it is not funny. The objective evidence of Balmes and the scholastics merely said that certitude was warranted when the thing itself imposed itself on knowledge. It was not my incapacity to deny that made the assent certain, but rather the object itself imposing the need of assent. Whenever the object was assimilated, the assent was certain. However, with this formula the problem is not satisfactorily solved, but merely postponed. How do I know that I have assimilated the object? The answer will always be the same: in intuition it is impossible not to achieve it, and in all other forms of knowledge, because they are knowledge forms, the presumption is that it has been reached. There is only that presumption. On the grounds of that presumption the elements common and perduring to all empirical knowledge of the empirical object in general are reductively certain with the certainty of intuition, because if the common and perduring were not real, then the empirical observation would not be a knowledge form—but it is by intuition. Hence, the whole doctrine of evidence, whether in the Cartesian or Balmesian form, is not the last word on the subject but rather a superficial first word.

Summary

We may now summarize our investigation of the question of certitude.

(1) Just as knowledge is a fact, so certitude is a fact at least as a state.

(2) Certitude is not a univocal term. There are at least three kinds of certitude.

(3) Absolute or perfect certitude is possible only on the level of consciousness and on the level of metaphysical intuition because the real is assimilated in itself, and since certitude is nothing but the tranquillity of truth achievement, the certitude is here inevitable.

(4) Imperfect or prudential certitude accompanies a spontaneous assent of the knowing faculty on the empirical or faith plane, when no positive motive is given to withhold assent. Such an assent is subsequently reformable; it will never be entirely wrong. The justification of such assent is double: (a) on the plane of action which is necessary for life some assent is needed, (b) the knowing faculty is of itself capable of achieving the real and its spontaneous activity is in accord with its intuited movement toward truth. Working spontaneously and naturally it will reach the truth at least by approximation.

(5) Where error is probable, there will be no spontaneous movement toward assent.

(6) The elements common in the individual's perception of the empirical in general, coupled with the perception of others, will be reductively of the absolute order, for if these elements were wrong, then the knowing faculty would not be such, but it is given in intuition that it is a knowing faculty.

(7) There is no difficulty calling evidence in the Balmesian sense the motive of certitude in metaphysical intuition and consciousness, for where there is intuition the thing in itself has been seen.

(8) In the other forms of certitude the motive is the spontaneous going to the truth on the part of the knowing faculty, which is an object of intuition. The object is not seen but reached in terms of the seen. This motive can be called dynamic evidence, and thus more than mere animal faith. But error is possible and greater approximation to fuller truth is always possible.

(9) The reformable character of empirical knowledge never deprives it of a nucleus of irreformable truth.

(10) The reformability is indefinite since the individual essence is not known, and being unknown can always be proposed in a way of doing more justice to the individual essence that is the unreachable goal of knowledge of this kind of object.

In the light of these observations we can say that the discussion of certitude has been obscured because there was an unconscious attempt to reduce all certitude to one univocal kind. Descartes was looking for metaphysical certitude in all forms of knowledge, which is impossible. The scholastics were too much influenced by Descartes and, although they saw that certitude was different in different levels of knowledge, yet they were too much taken by the Cartesian stand to overcome the Cartesian urge to make all certainty apodictic.

The fideism of Lamennais and Malebranche was a reaction to the rationalism of the eighteenth and nineteenth centuries. To the extreme thesis of rationalism, namely, that on all questions we can achieve truth by the use of reasoning, they said that on no transcendental question can man achieve truth unaided by communal consent directed by God. The truth lies in the middle. Reason cannot do all things and the individual can do some things.

A Note on "Free" Certitude

A phrase has entered into scholastic circles which is strange to the ear, but quite satisfactory to the mind. To call certitude "free" is the same as calling pain "free." Certitude is the satisfaction felt by the subject when he has reached truth or thinks he has reached it. Such a feeling is no more free than any other feeling, but is automatically given. What the phrase means, of course, is that where there is no intuition, assent is not necessary and can be withheld. That does not mean that such an assent is chosen. If no reflection is made on the object under empirical observation, the knowing faculty spontaneously gives some assent, and even when there is reflection not all assent is open to suppression. When there is empirical perception, the knower must assent that he has perceived something. He is only free on more precise categorization.

However, in the matter of precise categorization no necessity is imposed on the thinker. If reflection takes place on this fact, then a free choice is made, and being free, it falls into the ethical field and can be judged in terms of culpability and innocence. It certainly is an act of responsibility. Error certainly is never necessary and is always free, though not ethically free unless reflection accompanies the final assent.

That the will does enter into assent is quite clear from experience. We do make assents that were not dictated by the truth, as is evident in all cases of error. The intellect only assents necessarily where truth is imposed. How can the will make the intellect assent? Because of the value or goodness of the assent. A critical moment in life demands action and action demands an intellectual stand, for we are intelligent agents. The goodness of a certain action will attract the will in such a way that it will allow the intellect to attend only to the factors in the total problem which will make possible an assent attracting the will. This is not done by some influence of the will on the intellect, but of the total agent who wills and thinks. Through his will a man acts; by his action which is thought action, he achieves a good. The whole process is not clear in detail but clear enough in outline.

Not all willed thinking is wishful thinking, nor even rationalization. Often enough by reflection the intellect sees that a certain assent is warranted by the object as presented in empirical observation, though the fallibility of concrete empirical judgment is always recognized. Such warranted assent is certain, but with that prudential certitude characteristic of the empirical level. Such assent can be corrected and will be corrected as experience and reflection demand. The absence of total security in such knowledge merely shows the limits of this kind of knowledge and not its invalidity.

4

*Thought
and Thought
Disciplines*

There is a great deal of needless misunderstanding and snip-
ing between the average man of common sense on the one
hand and the scientist or the philosopher on the other, or between the philosopher and the scientist, and so also for all the
various realms of thought. This is due to the failure of one or
both sides to understand what each is trying to do, what is the
precise object that he is considering, and what is the method
that he chooses in dealing with his object. All thinking is not
cut from the same cloth; there is a difference in the material and
in the quality of the process. The man of common sense, the
physical scientist, the historian, the sociologist, the mathematician, the philosopher, each chooses for his consideration different aspects of reality and proceeds by a different method.
Each may present a truth about the reality with which he deals.
It will not be the whole truth but only the truth able to be
achieved by that approach. One cannot do the others' jobs.
The scientist, as scientist, cannot do the philosopher's job; nor
the philosopher, as such, the scientist's job; nor can the average
man of common sense do either the philosopher's or the scientist's job.

There are some scholastic philosophers who, in a boastful
way, speak of scholasticism as the philosophy of common sense.

For them this is a recommendation of the type of philosophy they pursue. William James accepted this characterization of scholasticism and described it as common sense become pedantic. For him this was equivalent to a rejection of scholasticism. If there is any truth in the phrase, "the philosophy of common sense," it can only mean that scholasticism does not deny what is basic in common sense. There is undoubtedly a value here, for if we were right in our analysis, knowledge on any level achieves truth according to the limits of the level. However, no philosophy can be common sense. If it were, it would cease to be a philosophy, and scholasticism as proposed by its best representatives certainly moves far away from the vision of the world as constructed by common sense.

We propose to deal with three kinds of thought, the thought of common sense, which is undisciplined thought, and then two kinds of disciplined thought, that of the physical sciences and that of philosophy, in order to explain the object of each, its method, its value, and its limitations.

Common Sense

What is common sense? It indicates the intelligent procedure of a prudent man prescinding from all schooling or discipline. How does such a man proceed? He takes his thought instruments for granted; he does not reflect on them. He makes no criticism of their limits and objectives. He is more interested in action than in thought, and uses thought to make that action more valuable and satisfactory. Even his ethical conceptions are never rationally achieved, though they may be intelligently sustained.

Such a man, a rare jewel in any time, and rarer today when science has replaced common sense knowledge in so many fields, uses his thought processes promiscuously. His scheme of the real is partially derived from metaphysical intuition, though faith plays a more important part. He reasons without ever having examined the role and limits of reason. His ethical norms influence his judgment; the modes and superstitions of the age are premises to conclusions no less than empirical observation, to which he gives the most importance. Cultural thought patterns which are mythological frameworks for knowledge in a given time and place are taken literally as the framework of the real.

To ask common sense to lead us to the heart of truth is to ask the impossible. Common sense will contradict any new formulation of experience and of metaphysical intuition. By common sense the world is flat, a notion that philosophy for more than two thousand years rejected and which science has thrown into the discard for four centuries. By common sense the redness of the rose is perfectly similar to the perceived redness of the image of the rose. Yet science teaches clearly that objective redness is energy proceeding from the rose to the psyche where it is expressed in the red perception image. Image and energy are of different orders altogether. Common sense only a hundred years ago dismissed the possibility of iron ships because common sense knew from experience that iron sinks. Common sense, having been rendered familiar with telephone and television, says that it hears John Jones talking and sees him walking, when the fact is that it gathers up in sound and vision images an energy pattern attached to the speech and action of John Jones. Common sense tells us that a multicolored arch spreads over the earth when sun and rain coincide, but the truth is that no such arch rests on the earth but is a phenomenon of light.

Common sense is useless for telling me what the more intimate nature of things is. It cannot do more than present the grosser aspects of reality in a gross way. It is no argument in philosophical discussion, which latter tries to penetrate beneath the gross. It is perfectly valid as a norm for prudent human action and will have some value in the formulation of general principles of ethics. Outside that field its value is very slight indeed.

However, we must not go to extremes. Common sense must not be summarily dismissed as a complex of the Freudian concept of the unconscious, popular superstition with no valid insight, wishful thinking, and childish fantasy. Common sense is the unreflective use of any and all thought processes. Because it is unreflective it can use a thought process beyond the limits of the process, because such limits were never studied since no reflection took place. Error is easy by this method. Yet as we have seen, no thought process is entirely fallacious. Some truth is always ascertained, though it is not clear at any moment how much is truth and how much is error. A conflict between common sense and the findings of some disciplined thought does not warrant the simple rejection of common sense. Reflection is necessary to see where error lies. Common sense did perceive something, and if this something is denied by the findings of the discipline, it was the discipline that erred and not common sense. When John Watson, in the name of scientific psychology, insisted that thought was only silent vocalization and that beyond this there was nothing, that thought resided in the vocal cords and not somewhere else, common sense rebelled, and today thinkers accept the revolt of common sense rather than the findings of John Watson.

We may safely say that common sense is no guide to the intimate knowledge of the real. It is an excellent guide for prudent action, general ethical principles, and the grosser aspects of the empirical real. Beyond that it will not go. It also has a vague veto power, because it is not totally fallacious and some element derived by common sense is real. No disciplined thought by the mere title of discipline can override the veto of common sense in this vague field.

Disciplined Thought

From the earliest times there was thought discipline, i.e., thinking according to a method. The Egyptians had rules for measuring land, and these rules were the result of thinking. They had science and a religious philosophy. The ancient Romans and Greeks developed legal codes and applied thought to communal action. The ancient Chinese applied thought to ethics. In all such application thought was controlled by a set subject. Analysis and reflection went on, but the rules of thinking in these fields were not clearly expressed.

The Greeks had a special interest in this kind of thinking and developed a conscious method for it, whereby it could be controlled. The Aristotelian logic was an expression of the method and control. Methodical and controlled thinking is disciplined thought, the purpose of which is to answer the second question that is a real question in epistemology: "how can error be avoided?" We shall first investigate the thought discipline of science and then the thought discipline of philosophy.

Science

Origins

Words are human things and like human things they undergo change. Science or *epistéme* had a definite meaning in the time of the Greek thinkers. It meant for Plato what is usually today called philosophy, and what today is called science was explicitly declared by Plato not to be science at all. Aristotle, being an empiricist at heart, joined the modern notion of science to the Platonic notion and therefore science for him included both philosophy and science. This notion carried on through Western culture until the sixteenth century. In the East it was not developed at all, for scientific thinking as far as the orientals were concerned was not important. The important thinking was ethical thinking carrying over into life, and such thinking is generally called wisdom. Action is considered so that it will be ethically good action.

There are four names which are connected with the birth of science as a thought discipline distinct from the philosophico-scientific discipline that prevailed from Thales to William of Ockham: Nicholas Copernicus, whose *De Orbium Coelestium Revolutionibus,* dedicated to Paul III, was published posthumously in 1543; Francis Bacon, 1561-1626; Galileo Galilei, 1564-1642; and Johann Kepler, 1571-1630, who used the observations of Tycho Brahe, 1546-1601.

These names of the sixteenth century represent most of Western Europe: Poland, Italy, England, Germany, Denmark. These men lived while Christendom endured, in a united Western Europe where religious faith and religious obedience to Rome were the source of union. However, from 1450 onward something new was sweeping over this part of the world, and this new thing came from Italy. We call it the Renaissance. Greek literature was read avidly and its naturalistic philosophy influenced the European mind, turning it away from the Christian vision which had its noblest expression in the *Summa* of Saint Thomas in the thirteenth century and in literature in the *Divina Commedia* of Dante Alighieri. That vision had not evolved because it was a fairly complete thing. The passing times made the vision static and sterile and the expositors of the system simplified it by making it nominalistic, i.e., verbal formulation following a crossword puzzle technique. It was therefore no food for the mind seeking the real.

In the meantime the real was being perceived in novel form. The classical literatures were read and the goodness of earthly things was perceived. The ascetical color of Christianity had robbed the material of legitimacy. Sin was well known but innocent enjoyment was less approved than renunciation. Pleasure was a tainted thing which asceticism considered bad. Cristoforo Colombo discovered the Indies in the West and Fernão de Magalhães, 1480-1521, went around the globe seeing new things. Men of the Iberian peninsula opened up a large world to Europe, a world with strange peoples living in strange ways. The Christian scheme was far too simple to explain all this, and much that had been taught was clearly false. There were antipodes, though the learned had denied it. There were many peoples and Christianity had actually touched only a small percentage of the totality of the human race. The smug belief that the world was Christian or that Christianity had been preached everywhere was now shown to be false. In most parts of the world life was led in a way very distinct from the image held by Europeans of the West. It was no longer a question of Christians and Moslems. Together, they were a small factor in comparison with the many who were neither one nor the other.

There was only one way to learn about all these new things. One had to look at them. The Aristotelico-Scholastic vision was not ample enough to take care of it all.

The man who did the most to shatter faith in the Aristotelian image of the world was Galileo. His importance is seldom understood. This man, profoundly rational, attacked the real, not by fitting it into the Aristotelian scheme, but by building a new scheme. Needless to say he had all the learned men of his epoch and region against him. If Galileo was right, most of their learning was so much nonsense. No man will willingly believe this of his vision of the universe. What is more, they were in possession and Galileo was the aggressor and they were not ready to hand over the citadel without a struggle. As in the case of Socrates, so in the case of Galileo, the disgruntled philosophers decided to make Galileo retire from his position by accusing him of irreligion. They felt that they could win on this plane, for all religious thinking, theology, had been formulated along the Aristotelian philosophy. Galileo's appeal to a different framework would hardly be accepted in this tribunal. The Church, protector not only of the deposit of Christian faith, but also protector of Western cultural patterns, silenced Galileo. This silencing was only momentary, for his voice in the mouths of many others was heard everywhere. The Aristotelians, using the Church power as their instrument, could only fight a rear-guard guerilla campaign. The insufficiency of their image of the world was patent.

In England, Francis Bacon, with his English sense of the pragmatical and the empirical, repeated what Roger Bacon had said three centuries before, but he said it more lucidly and with an insight that he was opposing the Aristotelians. If Aristotle wrote an *Organum,* a scientific method, Bacon would write a *Novum Organum,* a new scientific method, the method of pure empiricism and not a mixed metaphysical empiricism. Francis Bacon was no scientist, yet he had accurate insights into the procedure of science which was actually being carried out in Europe.

If Galileo was the best expression of the new discipline because of his empirical approach, Kepler was the best theorist in the new field. He did not make observations, but using the data discovered by Tycho Brahe and the hypothesis technique illuminated by mathematics, he proved that the startling discovery of Copernicus was only half a discovery. The orbit of the earth around the sun was not and could not be circular in the light of facts and mathematics. It must be elliptical.

These four men changed the thinking of Europe. The discipline that was the only recognized one before their time, the philosophic, now gave way in popularity to the new discipline which was quite definite though not yet conscious of itself. Advances were made in every field, though the new discipline dealt primarily with physics. History, however, was growing simultaneously, thanks to the religious needs of the times. What the Fathers of the Church actually taught, how the primitive Church lived, what the Gospel story meant, were all questions that needed the new approach in history. Flacius Illyricus with his fellow Centuriators were opening the documents, and under their influence Cardinal Baronius was forced to do the same things.

The victory of the new discipline was decisive the moment that Cambridge produced the scholar Isaac Newton, 1642-1727. The Aristotelian image was definitely supplanted. The static earth as the center of a continuous material reality that was hemmed in by God, where things moved when pushed, or because they had been violently ejected from a definitely concrete place to which they wished to return in terms of lightness and heaviness, gave way to an open universe, where things moved or were at rest until changed by a force. Stability was gone. Movement took its place. Mathematics of space took the place of metaphysical consideration of abstract being as a principle of coordinating observed data. The real was no longer intelligible but observable, and coordination was made in terms of economy and postulate, and not by an a priori metaphysic.

The Newtonian image dominated the thought of the West until the twentieth century when Einstein re-examined the image and made it more simple. He simplified it by making conscious use of the principles that Newton used spontaneously. This brought about the necessity of thinking about science and this work has been done with great fruitfulness in the last fifty years. Today we are in a better position to know what the scientific discipline is than ever before. Let us begin by a descriptive analysis of what the scientist does.

Method

The scientist observes reality on the empirical level. This is always the first step; no other step is prior to it. His observation may be of two kinds. He may simply look on the empirical object without modifying it in any way or he may modify it and observe it in its modified state. His observation is not the casual stare of the passer-by, but an orderly procedure. It is rendered orderly by being exact, and exactitude is attained by observing it in relation to a standard usually conventionally chosen, which means measuring.

Observation. There are three laws of all observation:

(1) It must be objective, i.e., the description must be in terms of the thing and not in terms of the affective reaction of the individual who observes. "The cruel, crawling foam,"

as Ruskin pointed out in Kingsley's poem, is a pathetic fallacy. The foam is neither cruel nor crawling. The poet spoke of the foam as if it were a person.

(2) It must be accurate, i.e., it must describe the object so that it stands out in its proper and precise reality, leaving no hazy or fuzzy edges which dim the limitations of the thing.

(3) It must be exact, i.e., the accuracy must be mathematically determined.

These three requisites are achieved by measuring the object. Measure means referring the object to a conventional norm which is objective. In the present this norm is the MKS system —meter, kilogram, second. A meter was originally defined as one ten-millionth part of a meridian that passes from the pole to the equator. This was reproduced in platinum on the official meter stick preserved in Paris. Although it was subsequently found that this meter stick was in error, still the stick was used as the standard.[1] A kilogram was originally defined to be the weight of pure water at its greatest density temperature at sea level in the volume of 1000 cubic centimeters, which volume is called a liter. The platinum model for the kilogram was later discovered to differ minutely from the weight of 1000 cubic centimeters, but by international convention the platinum model was adopted as the standard. The second is one three-thousand-six-hundredth of a twenty-fourth part of a period of the earth's rotation on its own axis. These conventional terms, sheerly objective, are used as the standards of reference whereby a thing is observed. Other norms are established conventionally for other things such as ohms, volts, watts, etc.; however, all have their basis in the MKS system.

We see then that the objectivity of scientific observation is achieved by *measurement*. In other words, science deals with

---

[1] The new definition of the meter, adopted in October 1960, is 1,650,763.73 wave lengths of the orange-red light of Krypton 86. This permits an accuracy of one part in one hundred million.

the measurable and for this reason mathematical number is the true language of science. Scientific observation is made in terms of space and time and motion.

There are two kinds of observation:

(1) Observation without modifying the object observed. This is direct observation and we have excellent examples of this in astronomy, in seismology, and in the observation used in biology and geology, which serves as a kind of measurement, though not strictly so.

(2) Experiment—in which the object is modified and observed in its modified state. This is a torturing of the object; it is forced to react in circumstances that do not spontaneously surround it. This kind of observation is very necessary, for unless we see the object acting in many circumstances, we cannot tell all that it can do and therefore all that it *is*. Nor can we wait until certain circumstances occur spontaneously, for this wait may be too long, or the circumstances may never occur. What an animal will do in a germ-free environment is something that nature will never show us. We must modify the environment because nature will never do it.

Experiment. The two kinds of experiment are:

(1) Directed experiment—choosing a definite environment for the object in order that the observer, because of some special interest, may see what it will do in this environment rather than in another. Thus the chemist in analysis modifies the object along a line which will manifest if it contains this or that element whose presence or absence is of interest to him.

(2) Casual experiment—putting the object in different environments without being interested in one environment rather than another in order to see in general all the properties of the object. Thus the vulcanization of rubber was discovered casually by Goodrich, for he did not intend to

apply heat to rubber treated with sulphur, but a piece fell accidentally on a hot stove. Thus too, the Nazis experimented with human beings by exposing them to extreme heat or extreme cold, just to see what the reaction would be.

In all experiment instruments are used. These were formerly called philosophical instruments or apparatus in the days when science and philosophy still were confused. These instruments are of three kinds:

(1) Instruments to expand the powers of observation which are limited by nature. Thus a microscope or telescope is used to expand the powers of the eye. The stethoscope is used to expand the powers of the ear.

(2) Instruments of measurement. The simplest instrument of measurement is the yard or meter stick. A balance is a similar instrument. A photometer is more complex. All these instruments are of two kinds:

   (a) measuring instruments which do not measure automatically but rather require the observer to measure by observing the measure and the measured simultaneously. A yardstick is such a measure.

   (b) measuring instruments which measure the measured automatically. Thus a speedometer gives me the speed of the car without my doing any calculation, which is all done by the measuring instrument itself.

(3) Instruments to change the environment of the object. Wires carrying electric current are attached to a Geissler tube to ionize the gas contained.

Many of these instruments are ingenious and show much thought. In most observation the excellence of the observer consists not in observing, which almost anyone can do with a little training, but in the conception of an instrument which will bring out a new phase in the activity of the object or reach a phase but dimly perceived. The observer who devises such instruments achieves some degree of immortality in the history of science.

Hypothesis. After observation the next step in the scientific method is the hypothesis, i.e., a supposition tentatively presented as the explanation of the phenomena observed. As Francis Bacon pointed out, the mere observation of nature does not of itself give us satisfaction. He identified knowledge with power. If I can make nature obey me, if I have power over nature, then I can be said to know. It was therefore necessary to know the active principles in the object which were at work in the phenomenon. This was not given by the object as observed. These principles must be derived by reason.

Now Bacon in his scientific method supposed that certain rules of induction would indicate these principles. He spoke of the three processes of inductive thinking: presence, absence, and degrees. John Stuart Mill, 1806-1873, in his work, *A System of Logic,* used the same three steps and added a fourth with these names: agreement, difference, concomitant variations, and residues. Mill, like Bacon, explained things by what they called "cause," which is not at all what Aristotle or Thomas meant. In Mill it means only the active determining principle in the thing, and for him the principle of determinism and the principle of causality are identical. In the method of agreement b is observed as always following on a, and a is then called the cause of b. All those on a picnic who contracted food poisoning had in common that they had eaten mayonnaise. Therefore it is inferred that the mayonnaise is the cause of the food poisoning. In the method of difference b is never present when a is absent, hence a is the cause of b. At the same picnic those who did not eat mayonnaise did not contract food poisoning. Therefore the mayonnaise is the cause of the food poisoning. In the method of concomitant variations the observer notes that b is present in proportional degrees identical with the proportional degrees of the presence of a, and hence the cause of b is a. Silver nitrate is deposited on a photographic negative in proportion to the amount of light admitted. Hence the reduction to silver nitrate is caused by light. In the method of residues, if the observer sees a complex of phenomena, x',y',z',b, and he has a complex of antecedents, x,y,z, and a, and knows that x is the cause of x', and y is the cause of y', and z is the cause of z', then a is the cause of b. A classic example of the use of this method in the field of chemistry is the discovery of the chemical element, argon, by Rayleigh and Ramsay in 1894. It had been observed that nitrogen obtained from chemical compounds invariably weighed less than nitrogen obtained from the atmosphere. The residue in weight eventually led to the hypothesis that atmospheric nitrogen was mixed with some other element. Further experimentation led to the isolation of the new element, argon, the weight of which accounted for the residue.

Now in the mind of Bacon and Mill the cause, i.e., determining principle which "explains" the phenomenon, is given by sheer observation, and observation induces the induction spontaneously. Of course a difficulty at once arose which Anthony Standen[2] has wittily expressed in the following story: Jones drinks scotch and soda on Sunday and he gets drunk; on Monday he drinks gin and soda and he gets drunk; on Tuesday he drinks brandy and soda and he gets drunk. On the Millsian logic, if superficially applied, the conclusion is that Jones got drunk on the soda.

There is, however, a more serious difficulty raised by this witty objection. Mills would answer Standen by saying that his story shows poor control of the inductive apparatus. The alcohol was always present on the three occasions. This is true, but when can we be certain that we are not being superficial?

Another difficulty which is more devastating is that planned

---

[2] A. Standen, *Science Is a Sacred Cow* (New York: E. P. Dutton & Co., Inc., 1950), p. 25; also published as a Dutton Everyman Paperback.

experimentation cannot be explained by this kind of induction. What would make the experimenter do one experiment rather than another? He must have some clue, or otherwise he would not do this experiment rather than the other. What is more, the great discoveries in the field of science have not been made by following the method of Mill. Therefore, Claude Bernard,[3] 1813-1878, and after him Henri Poincaré, 1854-1912, and Edmond Goblot, 1858-1935, inverted the order of Mill. It was not the experience that engendered hypothesis, but hypothesis that makes possible experiment. The scientist has a clue, an insight, and because of this he tries it out. Where does the clue come from? From a *vis imaginativa,* the genius in the scientist. It is this that makes the great scientist. He has an "intuition." This is not a guess, but rather a rapid analytical ratiocination of a synthetic insight aroused by the data already achieved. He tests it experimentally and experience shows him to be right or wrong. This is the hypothesis method. The scientists suppose something to be true. This proposition will explain the data of observation and what is more, as a principle of deduction, it will permit the formation of conclusions that have not yet been observed. These conclusions suggest the crucial experiment, for if the experiment shows that it is so, then the hypothesis is accepted as "law."

This theory is accepted today by all. There is no Millsian vision of law rising full-panoplied from mere repeated experiment. The most that his logic will do is serve as a technique for verifying the hypothesis. Even here he is transcended. One experiment suffices; they are not multiplied. In this way Planck, Einstein, Heisenberg, Russell, and the others talk.

Summary. Hence we can say that the method of science proceeds through these steps:

(1) Initial direct observation, coupled with some casual experimentation;

---

[3] *La Science expérimentale* (Paris: J. B. Baillière et fils, 1878).

(2) The formation of the hypothesis which claims to propose
     the cause, which means the principle of determinism;
(3) The verification (or rejection) of the hypothesis by di-
     rected experiment;
(4) The formulation of the law.

Law—Image—Definition of science

Hypothesis and theory are interchangeable words. If a distinction is to be made, we can say that an hypothesis is a provi-
sional explanation without more recommendation than that
it would explain many of the known facts of a phenomenon.
If there is some experimental verification, i.e., deduced conclusions of the hypothesis are actually found in nature, then we
have a theory. If the theory is an explanation of a part of a field
of phenomena, it is a particular or special theory. If it covers
all the phenomena and reduces them to one explanation, it is
a general theory. Thus Einstein's Special Theory of Relativity
(1905) was first proposed to explain the electrodynamics of
bodies moving relative to one another with *constant uniform
velocity,* whereas, in his General Theory (1916) he wishes to
explain *all* relative states of motion, including non-uniform or
accelerated motion.

A law differs from a theory in as far as it is verified by crucial
experiment and is generally accepted. This does not mean that
it is irreformable. Laws are accepted not only because they are
verified but also because they are simple. An explanation that
contains less factors than another is a better one on the principle of Ockham's razor: *entia non sunt multiplicanda sine neces-
sitate.*[4] Likewise, the easier coherence of one law with already
known laws is a recommendation for reform. Consequently
verification is not the only justification of a law; simplicity and
coherence are also titles to be considered. However, the fundamental empirical character of scientific work merely demands

---

[4] Entities, or in this case causal factors, must not be multiplied without
necessity.

one condition: the explanation must be empirically verifiable *at least in principle*. An explanation which on principle admits no empirical verification must be rejected by the general principles of science.

Is the work of the scientist finished with the formulation of laws? Not at all. He wishes to use his laws so as to form an image of the whole empirical cosmos. Such an image was formerly a picture; today, however, the image is sheerly intellectual to be expressed in equations that indicate relations. The dream of science is to explain the universe in a single equation.

Why does the scientist wish to present an image of the cosmos? There is a difference of opinion. Men of the pragmatic mind want such an image in order to predict; for them prediction is the great fruit of science whereby we are enabled to make the cosmos serve human desire. This was the notion of Bacon and it was shared by William James and John Dewey. For Werner Heisenberg and Max Planck and Albert Einstein this pragmatic aim is not appealing. For them the image gives an aesthetic satisfaction, and men go into the field of science for the same reason that others go into the field of literature or art. Prediction for these men is only a sign of verification and not an end in itself. Both views are actually entertained by scientists.

However, let it be clearly kept in mind that the scientist is not satisfied in explaining this or that type of action in the empirical universe. He wishes to explain the totality of phenomena with an adequate image, at least of a mathematical nature, where relations rather than substantial objects are exactly presented. The fact that such a synthesis seems difficult today because of the manifold fruits of scientific discovery does not deprive the scientist of the hope and drive that such a synthesis will be forthcoming.

In the light of the preceding analysis we can give a descriptive definition of science as it is. We make no judgment concerning what it should be. That our definition is adequate can be seen from the scientists who write about their discipline. The bibliography on the theory of science appended to this text will supply the testimonies needed.

Science is an intellectual discipline which proceeds from accurate, exact, and methodic experience on the empirical level to a rational and economic synthesis of determining principles in order to construct a mathematical image of the universe that will be both useful and satisfying.

Criticism

It is easier to describe what the scientist does than to justify his actions logically. The whole scientific procedure presents logical problems of the most trying kind. To many scientists it will seem strange indeed to think that he needs justification, though the best minds in the scientific field are well aware that there are logical conflicts in the very phenomenon of science. Most scientists never give these conflicts a thought. They take some initial stand which they may accept as true or as a working postulate and proceed tranquilly with their work. They can point to a fruitfulness which no other discipline has ever achieved. Because of science, mankind in a short span of two centuries has been relieved of many of the burdens formerly imposed by space and time. Scientific medicine has prolonged his life and indicated better food; it has lessened man's suffering from bodily disease. Mechanics and chemistry have given man some control of space and time with the locomotive, the automobile, the airplane, and the rocket. Electricity has given us the light and force that a highly productive civilization needs, and has given us the telephone, the radio, and television. Psychology and sociology have helped us to understand ourselves and to live more harmoniously and efficiently in society. The benefits of science have been spectacular and real and there is no end to what it can do. That its boons can be abused, as for example that its control over atomic energy makes vast destruction possible, is not to be blamed on science, but on the moral weakness of men and society. Although some scientists wish to make a scientific ethics, here they have failed egregiously. It is always true that science is a noble thing. It needs no defence and merits no attack. That science also gave birth to a philosophy called scientism is something accidental, and scientism must be met on the field in which alone it can live—philosophy— which is outside of the scientific domain.

However, a philosopher who by his vocation can and should examine all that is real, is justified in examining science as it is. Scientists themselves have done so, showing a philosophic spirit in so doing, and their findings and pronouncements will be most helpful to the philosopher.

Criticism from the Logical *Point of View.* First of all, what must we say about the empiricism of science which is the bed-rock of the whole discipline? We have already seen that the empirical achievement of the existent other is one form of intellectual procedure. Hence this is a legitimate beginning. The scientist is certainly free to restrict his discipline to one or two forms of knowledge. However, he overlooks one fact: *the empirical is not purely empirical; it is always rendered meaningful and communicable through class notions.* Since the scientist does not wish to use the class meaning as a source of deduction, he forms a class empirically and almost by conventional consent. For him the description of an object is always an appeal to experience, and the definition of the object is exclusively phenomenal. A man is not a rational animal but such-and-such a figure of matter with this or that behavior. The rationality of man is not a meaning that can be analyzed in itself, but a label, conventional, that is attached to a certain complex of behavior. Consequently the scientist has no difficulty in discussing the intelligence of an ape or a mouse. That such a proposition is meaningless in pure thought does not annoy him, because for him intelligence has another value. He may understand by it the capacity of solving problems that affect the agent's life.

As a matter of fact, the scientist has gone a long way to make his initial desire real. He has tried hard and quite successfully to eliminate any metaphysic in his description; however, he has not done so completely, nor can he. He must describe the object with a judicial proposition and the predicate must be a universal. He realizes this and admits that he is not interested in the singular. Mouse $X478$ is not studied because it is *a* mouse. Any light that can be gained by observing $X478$ is a light on *mice*. That he achieves light on mice by studying $X478$ is something he postulates. He does not wish to prove this postulate; he accepts it as certain. The day that he can do without the postulate, he will do so, but up to the present he needs this postulate and uses it. He supposes the validity of the method and the certainty of the principles around which the method is built. The most basic principle that he uses is the so-called principle of causality, which means that every phenomenon is related to an antecedent which determined the phenomenon to be what it is, and that this antecedent is as empirical as the phenomenon. This is not identical with the Aristotelian doctrine of cause, not even with the notion of efficient cause. It comes nearer to what is called the uniformity of nature, which means that nature always works in the same identical way. The scientist does not prove this nor does he wish to prove it. He postulates it. It is a universal principle and serves as a principle of deduction. He then argues in this way: $X478$ is a mouse. Proof: he has the complex of observable notes which conventionally puts him into the scientific mouse class. But all mice in the same circumstances must behave in the same way. Proof: the principle of "causality." Therefore, having $X478$ is the same as if I had all the mice there ever were.

The difficulty with this seemingly logical procedure is that "mouse" used as a conventional label for $X478$ is not the same term as "mouse" used in the minor where it is said that mice always act in the same way. The second word "mouse" indicates a true universal, whereas the first "mouse" is just an X as far as metaphysical mice go. The first "mouse" is equivalent to: let us call this a mouse rather than an elephant. But whether it is a true member of the metaphysical mouse class is something the scientist does not wish to discuss, because he eschews all metaphysical inquiry. Yet his conclusion is valid only if the observed mouse is really a member of the metaphysical class of mice. Reason will not work on singulars; it must work on universals, and *the universal is never empirical.* Yet if the scientist does not reason, he is only describing phenomenally singular things, even though he may group singular objects. Such a group remains only a singular thing. Nothing can be said about it except that it is so and so; not that it *must* be so and so, or that in the future other similar objects will be so and so.

Here we have the first inner conflict of science. By its pretension it cannot appeal to the metaphysical universal which is not observable, and yet when it reasons it uses the metaphysical universal, for otherwise it will make no progress in reason. In other words, the scientist simply cannot live up to his own profession. That he has rationalized away this impossibility by using a system of postulates in his work does not change the fact. The man who states that he will have nothing to do with metaphysics since it is a source of error, promptly uses metaphysically a set of postulates to come to what he calls truth. This difficulty is fundamental and it can have no solution so long as science wishes to restrict its work only to empirical judgment and ratiocination.

Criticism from the Psychological *Point of View.* This brings up the second difficulty of the scientific method. It can hold only for the empirical and only for the material empirical. By law it must describe exactly and accurately; such description, in its ideal state, is numerical mensuration and, in a less pure state, is the construction of conventional classes whose membership is determined by observable characteristics, e.g., the presence of a backbone in an organism or the presence of lacteal ducts in the female. What a backbone is and what a lacteal duct is must be decided conventionally. There cannot be a true numerical index, for the identification is made by function and not by movement in space. Anything that is not spatial, or has no function in space, cannot be discussed by science. How much of reality the scientist thus excludes from his field of research he does not know. He certainly must know that he excludes the primary condition of all knowledge, consciousness, which will not take on any description of class, except by metaphysic. If the scientist supposes that there is nothing but the material, he is no longer a scientist but a metaphysician with a doctrine concerning the nature of the real. If he refuses to enter into this question and simply states that only by his method can truth be achieved, he is taking a stand in epistemology which rejects the validity of all processes except his, and this epistemology is philosophy and contains a metaphysic. The only scientist who can be wholly happy in his findings will be a philosopher who declares that reality is only material and that class notions are pragmatic devices of the mind to control a pluralistic universe. His happiness comes not from his science, however, but from the coherence of his science with his philosophy. The non-materialist can and does use science, but it must always raise troublesome questions for him which he would rather not face. He can truly say that his science teaches no philosophy. He can truthfully say that science is indifferent to all philosophy and that its techniques and postulates do not commit the scientist to any philosophic position, but, as Lancelot Hogben pointed out somewhere, as a scientist he must work as if materialism and pluralism were right. For a man who is neither a pluralist nor a materialist such an hypothesis is uncomfortable. It is not surprising that science, at least in the eighteenth and nineteenth centuries, made materialists of its devotees and ceases to do so today because the whole basis of science is being questioned seriously.

Criticism from the Physical *Point of View.* There is another difficulty that arises from the first step of science: objective observation. The scientists themselves have evolved this difficulty and the whole indeterminacy doctrine of Werner Heisenberg and Pascual Jordan rests on it. Can there be objective observation? Does not the observer, by the very fact of observing, change the object he is examining? Is not this datum different from the object in its natural unobserved condition? To measure the amount of temperature he must apply a thermometer. The thermometer has its own heat, and contact with the object will impart the thermometer's heat to the object, or imbibe heat from it. The final reading will not be the temperature of the unmodified object but of a modified object. In objects which are macroscopic this slight variation can be ignored, but in the microphysical world it cannot. The cell in the microscope is being showered by more light than in its normal environment, and if it is not, it cannot be observed. The microscope trains an unusual amount of light energy on the object, and energy will change the object. When this happens to an electron, the electron is violently modified and is observed not in normal environment but in an environment of violence. What is more, since it is so small, it is not observed directly but in its effects on a photographic plate. What we then observe is the effect of the chemical change in the big grains that surface the plate as affected by an electron, never observed, in a state of violence. Speaking strictly, electrons are theory constructs. They have never been observed, and although *in principle* observable, can never be observed practically. Electrons are the rationalizations of certain observations but not the objects of observation. In other words, objective observation is never possible in the sense that the object is perceived in an unmodified environment, for any perception changes the object's environment.

Criticism from the Physical *and* Technical *Points of View.* Akin to the above difficulty is the well-known technique of correcting the observation. Curve graphs are in common use in science. Yet observation gives only disparate points and sometimes the points by themselves do not fall on the final drawn curve. The observer simply takes it for granted that the relationship of the points must describe a curve and draws it, even though this means dislocating certain points. Even if there is no dislocation at all, just because they are unconnected, many non-observed points are possible in between the points observed, and there is no ground in terms of observation to suppose that those points with the points observed really make a nice smooth curve. The curve was never observed. It was *constructed,* and the construction takes the place of the observed in ratiocination. The scientist must answer that only in this way can he make progress and that the points do suggest the curve to such an extent that only a quibbler would object to what he is doing. This justification is pragmatically valid, but it violates his first principle, namely, that only the observed can be affirmed. There is at work here an ignored principle: nature is harmonious in its activity. With that principle there is no need to quarrel, but harmony must be introduced into observational findings. It will not be found there without the introduction. Nature suggests to a harmony-loving man its harmony; it does not show it. Now this curve-making technique is universal in science. The scientists do it on every level. If the data of experience are not harmonious and symmetrical, the scientists always correct them, just as in practical life we reduce fractions to whole numbers and nineteens to twenties, because the decimal cipher is more harmonious. It is easier to say "in the twenties" than to say "twenty-seven."

Criticism from the Philosophical *Point of View.* There is even a more radical difficulty which only the philosopher can see. The scientist's claim to be objective is quite fallacious. He refuses to be objective. There is his strong point. He has restricted himself not to the object in itself but to the object as manifested by experience. Experience is clearly subjective and except in a subject it is meaningless. The scientist prides himself that he will not discuss the unknowable noumenon, i.e., the thing-in-itself. He discusses the knowable phenomenon and discusses it exactly in spatial and temporal terms. Space and time are obviously subjective frameworks, as Aquinas, Kant, and Einstein all agree. (Einstein's space-time continuum has about as much to do with space and time as sound has to do with its image on the movie film.) The much-vaunted "objectivity" of science is only accuracy in the description of an experience. The scientist is not even committed by his science to believe that there is something that corresponds in reality to his experience, and there have been idealists who were scientists. Today the prevailing opinion is that there is a reality that corresponds to the experience, but how this correspondence is to be understood, if it can be understood at all, is something on which the actual scientists cannot agree. Sir James Jeans is quite Kantian in his approach to the objective real. There is an unknowable and a rational object which produces in the mind a phenomenon—the scientist's object. Planck and Einstein do not like the Kantian doctrine and think that the experience in a vague and confusing way does speak of a reality beyond experience, which reality exists and somehow is caught up objectively in thought. Most scientists do not give the matter any thought and blissfully work as if the experience were noumenal reality, urged by no other knowledge than common sense, a very poor guide in this kind of investigation.

In other words, science which wishes to be unmetaphysical and objective, really is metaphysical and subjective.

The next thing to be discussed is the scientist's way of reasoning. His demonstration is quite different from the Aristotelian. We have already seen how it works. Scientific ratiocination of the strict type proceeds as follows: by applying all the postulates of the scientific procedure on the members of a conventionally treated group labeled A, A can be declared to have this or that characteristic and to manifest this or that relationship.

The whole dynamism of this process comes from the postulates. That object X belongs to a conventional group is the scientist's affirmation. The scientist simply says: let a group be formed in which object X must be considered to be a member. The group of members is given a non-denoting name label. This is voluntary. It cannot be wrong or right, because it is simply the act of the will.

Now all the work that the scientist is going to do from that point on depends on the body of postulates he uses. No one can say just what all these postulates are, though some are quite clear. As far as the analysis of meaning is concerned, the scientist has been quite ready to adopt the mathematical method of analyzing all possible implications of a concrete meaning or set of meanings. Whether or not meaning as presented by the mathematician is verified by the scientist in this or that object is something that neither the scientist nor the mathematician knows. The mathematician is not at all interested. He merely tells you all the roads that can proceed from one point, freely chosen, making a map on this basis. If the map corresponds to the region, if the roads in the country are good, bad, or indifferent, he knows not, nor is he worried. The scientist moving along does not know if he is on the road that he chose under the information of the mathematician; he just supposes that he is. Whether the map really corresponds to the countryside is a problem not raised, and it is simply supposed to be so by an act of fiat. If he reaches the point that he wants to reach, he thinks that is enough guarantee, and he will use the map that helps him to that end, even though the map might be quite fallacious. The fact that the scientist got to his point might be quite coincidental and because of no virtue of the map. But the scientist will go on using the map because it worked once. If it stops working, he will ask the mathematician for another map, which the mathematician can easily give him, for he can make maps without end, since he does not refer to the countryside but to the order of possibles around a freely chosen point.

This procedure is not humanly satisfying. The mathematician refuses to say if the map is objective in the concrete, and yet he is the only consultant on whom the scientist relies. His only control over the mathematical map is whether by following it, he reaches some point he wished to reach.

Let us exemplify this by the Einsteinian contribution. Many geometries are possible in mathematics. A geometry is only the derivation of spatial relations, given an initial set of postulates and definitions. These postulates are freely chosen, but consistent with all mathematical work. For measurement in a plane, a gauge will have to be selected and will have to be true to mathematical theory of measurement, which is quite different from physical measurement. The gauge will be a conic curve on which any two points will be the measure of distance. Now conic curves are many. Euclid, about 300 B.C., chose a peculiar form of conic, where two points established the curve, known as the parabolic curve, though this must not be understood according to the image of the parabola. Nicolas Lobachevsky, 1793-1856, chose the hyperbolic conic. Georg Riemann, 1826-1866, chose a conic which was an ellipse, with the result that a finite space would be unbounded. One result from the difference in the selection of the conic gauge is that for Euclid, to a given line only one parallel can be drawn through a given point outside the line. For Lobachevsky, numberless parallels can be drawn. For Riemann, no parallels can be drawn.

Now Einstein in his study of motion came to the conclusion that it would be more simple and more economical to suppose that Riemann had the geometry which would help to understand space and time. With this supposition he reduced the Newtonian laws to simpler equations and was thus a true scientist. Consequently, today a Euclidean image in terms of three dimensions for the understanding of the universe is rejected. A Riemannian image of four dimensions is used instead. This is no appeal to the imagination which goes on imaging in three dimensions. The appeal is to the mathematician's intellectual image of a four-dimensional object.

To declare the four-dimensional universe to be something observed is of course far from the facts. The truth is that Einstein and the scientists, all of whom follow Einstein, derive their image not from observation which has not done much to make the older observations invalid, but from the principle of simplicity and economy.

World images

Every man has some sort of world image or over-all vision of the cosmos which serves as a framework within which individual day-to-day events take place. The primitive with his animistic view and the modern scientist with his mathematical view both conceive of some matrix and the processes by which events occur within the matrix in order to explain the phenomena which they observe. The image will be a product of the particular culture of each and will change and develop with the advance of disciplined thinking within that culture. This development can be seen by comparing the cosmological images of Aristotle, Newton, and Einstein which evolved in our European culture.

Aristotle's World. This image with the Ptolemaic modification of the astronomy was valid from the time of Aristotle until the time of Galileo.

(1) There is a world. The scientist has confidence in empirical perception.

(2) The world is made up of substantial, subsistent bodies, so distributed that the stable, opaque earth is the center of a system of concentric, transparent spheres on which the heavenly bodies are attached. The spheres move as spheres, thus moving the heavenly bodies.

(3) Bodies are known intellectually through abstraction of their forms and species.

(4) For every body there is a natural place which geometrically could be located by Euclidean geometry, thus supposing an absolute space.

(5) Time is also absolute.

(6) There is no empty space. Nature abhors a vacuum.

(7) Bodies change in space and in quality.

(8) Bodies are at rest by nature, and if moved, they are moved by another.

(9) If a body is moved from its place, it returns to its place by the inherent qualities of lightness or heaviness, or at least seeks to do so.

(10) Light (color), heat, and sound are immobile qualities of bodies. Through immediate or mediate contact with a perceiver the bodies communicate the qualities or forms. There is no action at a distance, i.e., action without contact of bodies. Force is resident in the bodies, which must be active by the fact that they *are*. Not all change is spatial. Bodies fall into four ultimate genera—fire, air, water, and earth.

Newton's World. This image, the outgrowth of the new scientific discipline of the Renaissance, was presented by Newton at the close of the seventeenth century.

(1) There is a world. The scientist has confidence in empirical perception.

(2) The world is made up of bodies in a Euclidean absolute space with much empty space.

(3) Bodies are known empirically and in terms of their motion. They are not known by intellectual abstraction. (The image is thoroughly empirical and is not the half-hearted empiricism of Aristotle.)

(4) Body is matter and matter is measurable in terms of a determined standard. This measurement is called the mass of the body.

(5) Mass is inert. It is defined as the physical measure of a body's resistance to change of motion. It persists in a state of rest or of uniform motion unless a change is produced by an impressed force. Force is defined in terms of mass.

Force is mass multiplied by acceleration, or mass resisting change of motion.

(6) The average rate of motion of a body is measured by the distance divided by the time involved in the motion.

(7) Space is Euclidean and absolute.

(8) Time is absolute.

(9) There is a cosmic force, described as gravitational attraction, at work everywhere. Every particle in the universe attracts every other particle with a force which is directly proportional to the product of their masses and inversely proportional to the square of the distance between them.

$$F = \frac{K\,Mm}{d^2}$$

(10) Heat, light, and electricity are corpuscular. The axiom of action at a distance is practically discarded, although the ether would explain contact. The axiom that nature abhors a vacuum is definitely discarded.

This image was slightly modified by introducing the concept of energy, the source of force. Energy is the correlative of mass but not identical with it. The ether was also introduced into the space of the universe. The whole thing was utterly mechanical—matter and spatial motion explained all phenomena.

Einstein's World. This image is the current one and begins about 1915.

(1) There is a world. The scientist has confidence in empirical perception.

(2) The world is made up of a basic matrix in which events take place. Bodies are only observational events without or with a conscious observer.

(3) There is no Euclidean absolute space. Space is three-dimensional and relative to an observer.

(4) There is no absolute time. Time is the fourth dimension of events, necessitating a Riemannian multidimensional

universe rather than the three-dimensional Euclidean universe, though Euclid is valid enough for events on our human plane.

(5) The gravitation of Newton is not an attraction but acceleration caused by the only movement possible in the universe, curved movement. But the equation still remains $F = K\ Mm/d^2$ to a close approximation.

(6) No body is at rest. All are in motion.

(7) Energy is proportional to mass and mass is proportional to energy. According to the Newtonian image a body in motion possessed an amount of energy equal to one-half the mass of the body multiplied by the square of its velocity. In the Einstein image even a body at rest possesses energy, called rest energy, which is given by the formula $E = mc^2$, where c is the velocity of light. The speed of light is the observational absolute. Also, $m = E/c^2$.

(8) Movement is not merely spatial. Mechanism cannot explain the universe as a whole.

(9) The matrix of the universe is a field, quite real, though "immaterial." It is a continuum, knowable by four interdependent dimensions of time and space, finite and unbounded, studded by movement, and where two world lines of movement intersect, a material event is achieved to be recognized by an observer as mass or energy.

(10) The absolutes in the system are: empirically, the speed of light, approximately 300,000 kilometers per second (186,-000 miles); philosophically, the space-time continuum which is the condition and limit of events. The system is wrongly called "relativity", because it is a search for sure absolutes.

In this system the axiom, nature abhors a vacuum, has no meaning. The solid hard bodies have been dissolved into events, knowable by movement which is more than spatial, though always spatially conditioned. Action at a distance has no meaning; it is admitted that the attractive force of Newton does not exist. The space-time continuum is not hard matter or tenuous ethereal matter. It is the limiting condition of reality that manifests itself in intersections of curved motion. The limits of the universe are not given a geometric figure, though there is speculation about it. Some, such as Willem de Sitter and the Abbé Lemaître, hold that the universe is expanding, i.e., the limits of space-time are moving outwards.

By the method of scientific discipline the Einsteinian image is superb. It has simplified the preceding images, and in so doing, eliminated certain problems which arose from the image and not from the real. It can only be expressed validly in mathematical symbols, i.e., relational values. No attempt is made to say what matter is, and only the observed is entered into the image. There is no other metaphysic but the unavoidable metaphysic of mathematical logic. The whole work was done by an a priori selection of mathematical systems, subsequently verified by experience, though no scientist, not even Einstein, holds that such verification is infallible proof. All admit that this image can be simplified or modified.

We have in this image the two drives of the scientific discipline: empiricism and rationalism. The empiricism is fundamental, but clearly not the empiricism of "common sense." All the metaphysical value of the predicates is just eliminated. The real is the real as given in empirical experience and does not make any statement concerning the ultimate thing in itself. The rationalism is the dynamic, but it is not the rationalism of Descartes who believed that by reason he could detect the scheme of the real once and for all. This rationalism is nothing but the acceptance of mathematics where there is power of discovery attributed to it. Its value is that it analyzes any set of definable propositions and by analysis brings out the implicits. Einstein simply chose one analysis as singularly fitting to the real of observation. He did not abstract the theory from the observed, but made the observed intelligible by a pre-existent rational scheme. He does not know if the world is as he says it is; he merely believes that the relational pattern as presented by a Riemannian geometry is a good enough map of the real, though hardly a portrait. In his work, *The Evolution of Physics,* we read:

> Physical concepts are free creations of the human mind, and are not, however it may seem, uniquely determined by the external world. In our endeavor to understand reality we are somewhat like a man trying to understand the mechanism of a closed watch. He sees the face and the moving hands, even hears its ticking, but he has no way of opening the case. If he is ingenious he may form some picture of a mechanism which could be responsible for all the things he observes, but he may never be quite sure his picture is the only one which could explain his observations. He will never be able to compare his picture with the real mechanism and he cannot even imagine the possibility or the meaning of such a comparison. But he certainly believes that, as his knowledge increases, his picture of reality will become simpler and simpler and will explain a wider and wider range of his sensuous impressions. He may also believe in the existence of the ideal limit of knowledge and that it is approached by the human mind. He may call this ideal limit the objective truth.[5]

No one who is interested in thought as an achievement of the real can be perfectly satisfied with this image, not because it is not a beautifully consistent image, but because we are not at all in rapport with reality so that we can say we have grasped it. A game is being played with interesting rules and graceful movement. But the world is not known; all that is known is a rational coordination by a postulated propositional system of things that are seen in this subjective thing called experience. The terrible Thomistic urge to deal with the thing in itself is completely ignored and by most scientists declared to be illusory. It would be most unjust to say with some carping critics of science that it is nothing but the rationalization of a process

---

[5] Albert Einstein and Leopold Infeld, *The Evolution of Physics* (New York: Simon and Schuster, 1938), p. 33. Quoted by permission of the Albert Einstein Estate.

interested in the making of things. Yet when all is said and done, the best justification of science is that "it works." Nothing is really known. Experience, a subjective state, is rationally coordinated by postulates. This elimination of the thing in itself from physics is clearly stated by Eddington:

> I shall have to emphasise elsewhere that the whole of our physical knowledge is based on measures and that the physical world consists, so to speak, of measure-groups resting on a shadowy background that lies outside the scope of physics. Therefore in conceiving a world which had existence apart from the measurements that we make of it, I was trespassing outside the limits of what we call physical reality. I would not dissent from the view that a vagary which by its very nature could not be measurable has no claim to a physical existence. No one knows what is meant by such a vagary.[6]

Positivism and empiricism

There is even a worse phenomenon in the scientific endeavor. Basically we have empiricism and rationalism as accepted ultimate knowledge processes. Empiricism is no longer the naïve sensism of the English empiricists, in which true thought was filtered out. The new empiricism is more modest and more critical. But it does by approximation what the old empiricism thought it had done absolutely—the elimination of the metaphysical content of judgment. It is done by approximation because the modern empiricist has recognized the fact of meaning which is quite different from the mere presence of a subjective state with objective connections. It is, however, very interesting to see that he deals with meanings as if they were only semantic symbols, which is a full return to the old nominalism which denied that there was any truth to a general class concept. There are no true universal realities. Now in the history of thought it was discovered that such an explanation of meaning or universality simply would not meet the exigen-

---

[6] Arthur S. Eddington, *The Nature of the Physical World* (New York: Cambridge University Press, 1929), p. 152. Cf. also pp. 250-260. Quoted by permission of the publishers.

cies of thought as a phenomenon within the control of the thinker. It is true that the modern scientist is very wary not to make the old nominalist stand his own. He merely says: let us not be committed by the metaphysical content of knowledge, though it is quite evident that it is there. Some have declared that content to be an unavoidable infection of experience because of cultural influences, as if this explained something. Culture will give me language and it will shape me according to certain attitudes. It will not explain thought which, with logical priority, is before culture. It would be a poor appeal to heredity to say that our bodies are the product of environment, though it is certainly true that environment modifies the body. It is equally true that environment directs thought in one direction or another, but it is always thought itself which is directed, and thought has its own imperious structure before it can be directed. The metaphysical content of thought is there by structure and not by the modification of thought processes by elements outside of that process. This last affirmation will doubtlessly be denied by all empiricists, but their denial is most metaphysical, as the slightest analysis will show.

Again rationalism is back with us in just as tyrannical form as it was in the heyday of Cartesianism. It is no longer dressed as a Renaissance king, but like a sober bank accountant going over the books, spreading terror in all the employees of the bank or company, because there is no appeal from the accountant except to another accountant using substantially the same method. The accountant and the bookkeepers simply take it for granted that all entries must follow a certain pattern, and that the accountants know the pattern. That this has nothing to do with autos, potatoes, and tennis rackets is well understood by all, but tennis rackets and potatoes must fall into the accountant pattern. Anything that does not fall into the accountant pattern is not considered relevant. The possibility that there are values in the bank or company which cannot be included in the accountant's pattern is not entertained seriously,

though such a possibility is discussed by men who are not accountants. Bookkeeping processes may change, but only on
the accountant's leave. He controls bookkeeping and bookkeeping controls the bank and production. This rationalism is not
the rationalism of a metaphysical order. Logic alone is used.
However, the breakdown of the metaphysical rationalism came
about when it was recognized that much of reality had to be
grasped by means other than rationalism. The new rationalism
is subject to the same objection as the old one. Logic cannot
discover anything, as the empirical nature of science clearly
shows and admits. It has only veto power. Logic itself, however,
points to a knowledge other than logic which will not be expressed by logic, because logic depends on it. The attempt to
restrict all affirmation and all achievement of the real to the
logical plane of thought simply will arouse once more the revolt of Lamennais, Marx, and Kierkegaard, and in fact, the
revolt is with us in the more extreme kinds of existentialism
where the closed system of reason is simply rejected and an
anarchic state of things is put in its place.

Pure empiricism is meaningless. Pure rationalism is formal
and without content. The blend of empiricism and rationalism
which we call science shows that it was a creature of history,
when pure empiricism was rejected and pure rationalism abandoned, but not rejected and abandoned altogether. The blend
has value for the reason that it works, not because it is rationalism or empiricism, but because there is metaphysical energy
latent in the whole scheme.

Scientific recognition of inner tension

The first followers of the scientific method did not realize
that they had left the camp of philosophy. Both philosophers
and scientists thought that they belonged to one country. Hence
it was that the first scientists and later scientists, even as late as
the nineteenth century, thought they were giving ultimate answers to questions. Their propositions and conclusions were

handed out to the public as absolute truth. At the end of the nineteenth century and definitely in the twentieth, such pretensions were shed. The relative character of science and the approximational value of its findings were and are clearly recognized. However, there was, and is still present, a certain security with reference to certain postulates of science. The law of causality, which means the law of universal determinism of the present by the past along an irreformable pattern, was and is an instrument of scientific procedure. Werner Heisenberg by pure scientific process shook the tranquil faith of science in this principle and was backed by Erwin Schrödinger, Paul Adrien Dirac, and Pascual Jordan, all of whom belong to this century. These men proposed the principle of indeterminacy. This indeterminacy is of a double kind. One kind is admitted by all scientists today. The other is still being discussed.

There are really two kinds of laws in science, but neither is a law in the old philosophic sense. The philosopher, by using an anthropomorphism, called the principle of determination in physical reality a law, analogous to the determination given to a human community by a lawmaker. The scientist considers a law as a synthetic summation according to a rationale of a defined field of phenomena. The rationale has principles whereby the summation can be made. These principles are formal laws. They are not proved. They are not, in one sense, considered to be true, i.e., discovered. They are the structural principles of science. They are laws of method as applied to the field of science. These are always given as certain, though no objective certainty is attributed to them. They are certain as rational dynamisms in science. What the philosopher does with them does not interest the scientist. He will willingly drop any one of them if it makes his scientific structure simpler. Its truth or falsehood is no concern of his.

Besides these formal laws, whose validity is given and confirmed by the fact that by them the scientist makes progress through prediction, there are also physical laws. These laws are the summations of experience made into general principles of deduction thanks to the law of causality, i.e., the law of determinism. This states formally that any event is determined by a previous event in such a way that, given the previous event, the subsequent event is inevitable, and given the subsequent, the previous event was also present. This makes for the postulated uniformity of nature.

The earlier scientists thought that in this way they were announcing final laws, to be discarded only if experience showed them to be inadequate, always a condition in science.

However, as we saw in our criticism of the empirical pretension of science in its observations, the brute fact is not achieved ever. The event, observed in the MKS system, precisely because of that observation, is no longer the brute fact. Just how the brute fact is constituted in nature is something we can never know. The thermometer changes the temperature of the measured body. Small bodies, smaller than the cell of the eye and optical nerves cannot be held in check by the eye, because they flow through the sieve of cells that make vision. They can be studied, however, in those effects that can be seen, and for the unobserved brute event there is substituted a physical concept, let us say, an electron, a proton, a meson, a neutron.

Moreover, the Einsteinian identification of matter and energy, and the persuasion of scientists that energy and matter are discretely granular and not continuously extended, brought forth a startling discovery. The velocities of light and electromagnetic waves ever since the days of Maxwell were calculated on the basis that they were waves in an ether, for waves are not things in themselves but movements of a medium. The investigations of Thomson and Rutherford led to the notion that electricity and light were made up of little grains, which Newton before had called corpuscles. On the basis of this hypothesis light and electricity were not really waves but streams of grains. Yet the velocity of the corpuscle could not be measured because it could not be observed moving in its individual reality. It could only be measured in terms of the movement of a mass of corpuscles that acted as if they were a mathematical wave. Hence there became evident a simple truth: we can ascertain the position of an electron, but we cannot ascertain its velocity as an individual electron, and we can ascertain the velocity of a group of electrons if we treat them as a single wave, but in doing so we can never ascertain the position of a single electron. The wave describes the mean velocity and movement of many electrons. Being a mean measure of the velocity, it tells us nothing about the velocity of a determined electron. Now by the older physics of the Newtonian era it was necessary to find the position of an object and its velocity in order to know it. Mass was known by its inertia which was measured by a force. Both were manifested by motion which was known in terms of space and time where position and velocity had to be known. In the new physics all we could know was the occasional position of a particle and the speed manifested by a moving group of particles, where the speed was the mean of the discrete particles in motion.

The result was that the nature of the physical law was changed. It was no longer absolute for the individual particle. It was only possible to give a calculation of probability, worked out in the mathematical theory of probabilities, for the individuals. The nature of the physical law was *statistical*.

Statistical necessity is group necessity. Hence the law of causality was not violated but was rather referred to mass or group reality and no longer to an individual. For the individual, only probability was ascertained according to the proportions worked out by mathematics.

How this works out in the concrete can be seen by a rude example. Let us suppose that we know that 5,000 people pass through four turnstiles in a subway station but we cannot know which turnstile is used by the different people. Everything else being equal, each turnstile can be considered as having received 1,250 people. There is however no necessity that each turnstile received that exact figure. It really was possible that the 5,000 all passed through the same turnstile. This is possible but not probable in view of the other possibilities. The mathematicians have worked out the degrees of probability for all numbers of 5,000 for the four turnstiles. The degree of probability can be calculated exactly, but the only thing certain is the degree of probability, which is achieved a priori. Just what each individual did as he approached the turnstile we can never know, for we only know that 5,000 got tokens at the booth. If we make the thing a bit more complicated, so that it is easier to go through one turnstile than another, we lower the probability for the other turnstiles, but it could still be true that some of the 5,000 went through the more difficult turnstiles. We can only say what was probable, more probable, and less probable for different travelers postulating different conditions in the travelers.

That the laws of probability actually give us a good norm for the prediction of the future can be seen in the practice of insurance companies. They work with statistical laws. They know that, under the conditions existing in the last twenty years in a given cultural area, of 5,000 men who reached the age of thirty at the beginning of the period, 4,500 lived to be fifty. Given then the same area and supposing that conditions will not change substantially, the 5,000 now approaching thirty can be given insurance policies on their lives, so that 4,500 will pay for 5,000. In this way the insurance companies know exactly what is going to happen and they can arrange their policy prices so that they make money. They do make money on this basis, but they could lose money, speaking absolutely. Even if their probability actually works out, they never know which ones of the 5,000 will be in the group of 500 that will die before fifty, and it is immaterial to the company who they are, for each is treated as actually equal to every other in the group. However, the probability may fail. All of the 5,000 may die before fifty, and the company will not receive its money. The value of the meaning of probability is that certain eventualities can be discounted safely even though they be possible, because a certainty favors a mass fact. Hence science today demands only mass certainty for its findings and recognizes that nothing certain can be said for an individual event. That the sun may rise tomorrow in the west rather than the east is possible; it is, however, highly improbable and the possibility can be discounted in planning for the future.[7]

That this concept of physical law is different from the philosopher's concept of physical law is evident. In place of certain prediction, only probable prediction is possible. Yet there is some certainty, the certainty of the statistical law. The postulate of the uniformity of nature is still retained. All that is relinquished is the hope of finding the determinacy for the individual, not because it is not there but because we cannot observe the individual in his pure state in motion. Einstein and Planck both so understand science and reality.

Heisenberg and Jordan, however, do not understand it in this way. For them the indeterminacy lies not in our incapacity to observe the individual in motion, but rather in the capriciousness of nature. Nature is not uniform down on the microcosmic level. According to the quantum physics of Planck, a body has different energy-emitting and energy-absorbing levels, discretely determined. Energy does not flow from a particle in only one quantity or quantum, but in a restricted number of quanta, each a unit which cannot be broken down. It is like a slot-machine. It gives out money, but always in nickels, dimes, and quarters. It cannot give money out in nine cents, or in three and one-half cents. The flow is not the flow of continuous water from a nozzle but the flow of bullets from a tube. The bullets may be smaller or larger, but they can never be smaller than the smallest bullet, and never a fraction of the different-sized bullets in the case. According to Heisenberg and Jordan, there is no way of observing any uniformity

---

[7] Cf. Einstein and Infeld, *The Evolution of Physics*, pp. 310-313.

in this procedure. The body may emit a dime, a nickel, or a quarter, but like the gambler, we cannot know which. We cannot know, because in nature there is no *observable* determination to one kind of coin rather than another. Indeterminacy lies in observable nature and not in our incapacity of observing nature in regard to particles. Consequently nature in its microcosmic reality, the reality that is basic, does not conform to the law of determination.

This view is most upsetting. Some strange conclusions were derived. Eddington believed that at last science had a ground for free will. The more traditional scientists wished to deny the whole Heisenberg discovery. Einstein and Planck believe that it is only another proof for indeterminacy due to incapacity of observation, but not a proof for the inapplicability of the law of causality. There is nothing but confusion in the philosophy of science because of the Heisenberg doctrine.

One wonders, however, whether all this is not unnecessary. Heisenberg does not deny the statistical constant in energy emission and absorption. Hence some necessity is there. He founds the necessity of statistical necessity differently from the others, but he admits the fact. The principle itself is clearly a formal principle, and cannot be proved by science one way or the other, since that will be a metaphysical task. If some necessity is admitted, some kind of determination that makes for constancy and uniformity, if only that of statistical law, the principle has not been rejected. However, the rigid use of the principle is gone. It has been rendered evident by mere empirical observation that this principle is not as despotic in reality as was thought in the eighteenth and nineteenth centuries, a belief that was never shared by mankind at large or by the better philosophers of the perennial tradition. It is impossible for the non-scientist to decide what is the truth of the indeterminacy of nature on the level of observation, and he must let the scientists work out the problem as best they can.

General conclusions

(1) Science is a well-defined thought discipline in terms of empirical observation and rationalistic coordination.

(2) Its fruits have been excellent, and therefore it is a valid discipline.

(3) It labors from many intrinsic paradoxes, if not contradictions, so that it could hardly be used as the only thought discipline.

(4) It is not even the ultimate thought discipline, because it supposes prior thought disciplines.

(5) The use of the mathematics instead of metaphysic as the source of coordination has been a splendid achievement, but mathematics is only logic and in logic a whole metaphysic is contained, and therefore science's exclusion of metaphysics is not thorough.

(6) Metaphysic cannot be rejected because it is unscientific, any more than pears must be cast into the garbage because they are not apples.

(7) The scientist does well in following his discipline, but he should recognize it as valid on a limited field.

(8) The identification of knowledge with empirical observation is an arbitrary procedure, valid enough for a discipline by postulational procedure, but hardly evident as a general principle.

Philosophy

Aristotle

One of the oldest disciplines of thought is philosophy; however, in the form in which it is usually known we think of the discipline as brought forth by the Greek mind beginning with Thales in the sixth century, B.C. This discipline has gone through a long evolution and it is difficult to describe it succinctly and accurately. Thales, Anaximander, and Anaximenes used some empirical data in their thinking, although it was not strictly scientific, but rather common sense empiricism. Pythagoras certainly was less empirical and more mathematical. Plato was not empirical at all, though he was mathematical. Aristotle tried to blend apriorism and empiricism, but his empiricism was not scientific, but rather common sense.

From that point on the figure of philosophy is set. The struggle remains always the same: how much empiricism must enter into philosophy? This question already supposes that some apriorism is of the essence of philosophy. Even the Aristotelian definition of science (which for him meant philosophy and not the discipline we call science), the knowledge of things by their ultimate causes, has meaning in the Aristotelian system. It has no meaning outside of that system and we must therefore reject this definition as final or universal.

The glib repetition of the Aristotelian definition as if it were a self-evident thing does much harm to students. First of all, the key word "cause" is usually understood as Aristotle's efficient cause which the normal student understands vaguely because of empirical connotations. Now for Aristotle the efficient cause was not the all-important cause. The final cause with its correlate of formal cause was more important, and this is not understood by the average student till very late in philosophy. Secondly, a scientist would declare that by Aristotle's definition, the scientist is the only true philosopher because he looks for the ultimate determinants of things, and that is what the scientist means by cause. But it is certain that science is not that which down the centuries has been called philosophy. Thirdly, the whole Aristotelian cause theory was an *ad hoc* construction to enable him to justify his strange union of empiricism and apriorism, which union was a philosophical enterprise before the cause concept was even constructed. It cannot be insisted too much that the Aristotelian definition of cause is a begging of the question and valid only as a pragmatic indication of the Aristotelian method. Philosophy is bigger than Aristotle.

Aquinas

Augustine's thinking was a mixture of faith, empiricism, and apriorism. It was never pure in any of the three forms. Thomas did much better. He purified the notions and gave us something to work on. For him philosophy was the study of the real in terms of being. As this stands in Thomistic writings, it is at once Aristotelian and vague. It is Aristotelian because Thomas falls back on a basic distinction of Aristotle—act and potency as the principles of being—which worked out physically as causes. *Arche* (principle) and *Aitia* (cause) are related notions but not identical. *Aitia* is only the necessary manifestation of *Arche*, but *Arche* belongs to being. The definition is vague because being is a vague word in discourse, though clear enough in thought; however, being permits no universal use because it is transcendental, and therefore is not a true universal. It is an analogous term. In spite of these shortcomings, we can still say that Thomas' thought is clear enough. Philosophy deals with things according to the thought principles involved in the acquisition of the real. Thought principles are not empirical principles, and Thomas' philosophic dynamism is not empirical though, like his master Aristotle, he is more interested in experience than Plato who was a pure thinker.

From Thomas' time onward, we find persistent attempts being made to reject the Thomistic approach to philosophy. Francis Bacon, who was a philosopher and not a scientist, wished to make philosophy science. René Descartes wished to make philosophy mathematics. Immanuel Kant wished to make philosophy epistemology and ethics. Hegel wished to make it history. Today all positivists and empiricists wish to make it a mathematical logic at the service of science.

Philosophy and scientism

This last assertion needs amplification. The scientist, as we have seen, refuses to admit any discovery to thought except on the level of empirical observation. He admits that this will not give him a rational and general scheme. Hence he needs rationalization. However, he will not take it from the metaphysician who declares that his findings are real and therefore discoveries. The mathematician makes no such assertion. He simply deals with any proposition and shows the relationships implied therein and the relationships that arise when the proposition is juxtaposed with other propositions. He never deals with truth; he only deals with rightness of inference. He is a logician of a higher order than the Aristotelian logician who limited the field of logical inference to simple propositions. The prelogical foundation of logic is never touched by the mathematician nor is the empirical verification of mathematical findings his concern. That is why the scientist can consult him so willingly. He is only a coordinator. He makes no affirmation concerning the existential real and he refuses to accept commitments that come from beyond logic as a given thing. The metaphysician is not so indifferent to the value of his propositions. He insists on the real commitments implied by his propositions, and not only the logical ones. Hence the scientist can give him no right to do so.

Metaphysics

The soul of philosophy will be metaphysics. What is metaphysics? The word is most unfortunate and yet we are saddled with it. The word only indicates the treatise of Aristotle which in the Alexandrine edition of his works followed upon his physical meditations.[8] However, this treatise was what Aristotle called the first philosophy or theology. The nature of that treatise will give us a clue to the meaning of metaphysics, but only a clue, because a metaphysic can be conceived and expressed without taking on the Aristotelian mould. The treatise deals with being. Being means the verb or copula *is*. That this must be the first question in thought is clear from the phe-

---

[8] "Metaphysics" is from the Greek *meta physica*, meaning "after physics."

nomenon of communicable thought. All thought is meaningful by *is*. Without *is* no thought is meaningful. The primary meaning, therefore, must always be *is*, either in its participial or substantive form, *being*.

The truth of these ultimate assertions cannot be proved, because proof is always logical inference. Inference supposes some initial truth, for from it, it will infer. How, then, is the truth of the propositions derived? It can only be derived by an appeal to an analysis of thought as a given thing. In controversy we must simply force the adversary to make the analysis, which will be done by asking him the meaning of his words until he is forced back to the word *is*. Beyond that word, no questions are possible, for even "possible" is meaningful only by *is*.

Philosophy, therefore, is committed to the affirmation of knowledge on a prelogical and pre-empirical plane. Logical positivists will say that this is not knowledge but only intuition of formal mind structure. Santayana says something of the kind, although he gives reality to the ideal. Kant said exactly what the positivists say, and from him they took their position. However, these stands are mischievous. To call the use of the mind on the empirical plane the realm of knowledge and to deny the name of knowledge to the use of the mind on a more basic level is being capricious and childishly willful. The use of the mind on the basic plane will make possible the use of the mind on the next plane. Pure empiricism is not knowledge. It would only be an orgy of subjective sensation, without order and without value. The empiricist's escape by calling in the mathematician is only a half-way measure. The mathematician supposes as given that which the metaphysician analyzes. Mathematics will not escape metaphysic.

Therefore philosophy is primarily the discipline which deals with the a priori aspects of knowledge, and therefore with the real, for we have defined knowledge as the achievement of the real.

To discuss the real without recourse to philosophy is impossible. The primary aspects of the real are the field of philosophy, and without a knowledge of the primary aspects, nothing will be known, since these are the web of the real into which all else can be woven. This will be the true meaning of Aristotle's definition: knowledge of the real through ultimate causes, i.e., knowledge of the real in the light of its basic aspects.

How is this done in terms of the analysis of knowledge which we made? Philosophy certainly is not a discipline which restricts itself to the plane of consciousness, for that plane gives data but says nothing about them except that they are given. The primary aspects of the real are not given by empirical observation, because this type of knowledge, as we have seen, is meaningful by insights which cannot be derived from experiences. Faith is only empiricism at second hand. Hence the only field that is proper to philosophy will be the field of metaphysical intuition. However, philosophy does use reason, whether by mere rational analysis or true inference. Therefore philosophy works on the restricted planes of metaphysical intuition and reasoning, with the primacy necessarily given to metaphysical intuition.

The words "metaphysical intuition" are fighting words. They excite suspicion everywhere and in scientific circles arouse laughter and ridicule. However, these unpleasant reactions are not necessary and happen only because it is supposed that such intuition is uncontrolled guessing or wishful thinking. Any other word is welcome as long as it indicates that we are dealing with the knowledge or thinking about the word "being," or "real." "Metaphysical meditation" will be a nice phrase for it, though even "metaphysical" is a dangerous word. "Analytic investigation of the basis of all thought" will do very nicely because it seems to avoid fighting words. However, it must always mean that we are dealing with something that comes with experience but is prior to it in thought-commitments.

Metaphysics can then be defined as *the thought discipline that is concerned with the primary class concepts or quasi-class concepts of the transcendental order, in as far as they are reality.* Mathematics and logic also deal with these concepts— not in their reality but in their inferential fruitfulness. Both of these disciplines suppose something given as meaningful, though they do not discuss how these propositions acquired their initial meaningfulness, which always supposes that they were knowledge or thinking acts, and thus acquisitions of the real. Logic is the methodology of philosophy in its reasoning phase and mathematics is the methodology for all and any reasoning whether in philosophy or beyond it. Both are derived from the data of metaphysical intuition, the object of philosophy. In a true sense, mathematics is a division of philosophy, but it is not the first philosophy. Other disciplines that go beyond metaphysical intuition are no longer philosophy.

Metaphysics, however, can be an independent study or it can be applied to other subjects, given or supposed through experience or metaphysical analysis. In its applied form it will still be philosophy, but it will not be first philosophy. Philosophy is thus nuclearly metaphysics, but it can go beyond metaphysics as long as it deals with objects in the light of metaphysics, i.e., the primary phases of the real as given in the a priori grasp of it.

Empiricism and philosophy

With the previous affirmation made, there arises immediately the question of experience and philosophy. To make the discussion possible, let us speak of the data made manifest only in terms of the existent achieved in empirical observation. "There is nothing in the intellect which was not previously in sense," is an adage since the time of Aristotle. Leibniz modified the principle with the addition "except intellect itself." This modification did not intend to change the basic truth that Aristotle and his successors saw. The first experience can be discussed and can be discussed only because it was subject to category formulation, and therefore there was empirical data achieved and rendered meaningful by the categories. In other words, empiricism cannot ever be excluded from knowledge. Just as sheer empiricism is impossible, because the category comes with it, so sheer intellection is impossible because something of sense accompanies it. A "pure" philosophy is no more possible than a "pure" experience.

However, this empirical element does not vitiate the philosophic undertaking. Since the latter's true object is the meaning, the essence, the Idea, philosophy can deal with it immediately even though it was not achieved without some initial experience. That the experimental factor will influence the analysis extrinsically remains true. The value of the initial datum will depend on the physical and psychic constitution of the individual. His own environmental conditioning, his social background, his peculiar path through life, will show him some value in the object of contemplation that is unique and rational. The goodness of this or that meditation will influence him to make it, just as the evil of a different kind of analysis will deter him from making it. The old cry, "You think this way because your psychic urges lead you to it, or because your social conditioning makes it inevitable," is true but not as relevant as the champions of this kind of objection think. The supposed goodness perceived in a given reality impels a man to contemplate it, and contemplate it in such a way that it will manifest more and more the goodness perceived swiftly and without detail initially. A whole line of thought is excluded by this initial dictate. However, what is seen, is seen. That there is a danger that a partial vision will be sustained as a total vision is merely an error, profound perhaps, but only an error. The error was not in what was seen but in a rash assertion that in that vision all was seen. More experiences usually manifest the deficiency of a vision, but they can only show deficiency and not upset what was known. The man who urges that my Freudian complexes have colored my reasoning is speaking the truth, but he refuses to admit that such coloring really is an obstacle to the knowledge of the real, for he himself, when he has said this, thinks that he is in contact with my reality and objective reality, though he too is subject to the influence of Freudian complexes. If the analyst did not believe in the mind's capacity to render meaningful the aberrations of his patient, he could do nothing for him. Although the analyst speaks much of rationalization, he must reflect that it has meaning only if reasoning has meaning, for rationalization in the psychoanalytic sense is false reasoning, and if there were no true reasoning, there could be no false reasoning.

Hence there is always an empirical factor in knowledge, even the knowledge of the a priori, but this is not a contradiction. This only means that anyone's metaphysic has roots for its existence in the empirical, but its value is quite independent of that existence. That the full value of the metaphysical is not grasped by the individual is an existential fact. The metaphysician who thinks that his vision is better than another can prove this by forcing his hearer or opponent to widen his experience so that the more defective metaphysic will be incapable to render meaningful the real as experienced. This will demand a deepening of the metaphysic already achieved. It will not demand its rejection, for something has been gained. Certain unrecognized implicits will have to be made explicit; some identifications of the partial with the whole will have to vanish, but never does the whole of a metaphysical scheme have to be thrown away. In fact, nothing that is positive in it will have to be thrown away. Only negations will have to be transcended.

We have here a fundamental difference between the relationship of experience and meaning-intuition as it exists in science and in philosophy. The experimental is meaningful only by the metaphysical intuition, but the metaphysical intuition is valid in its own right, though bound existentially with an experience.

In the light of these general observations we can approach certain metaphysical assumptions made by thinkers. Aristotle believed that the inevitable linkage of intuition with experience meant that the object of intuition was contained in the object of experience. That is why he taught that the class concept was drawn from the individual. This is hardly plausible if taken strictly. The class concept cannot be verified in the individual, though it is true that, given classes, individuals belong to them. There was a slide from class to group in Aristotle's exposition of his thought, though he certainly was aware that he did not wish to speak of group, which is as singular as any individual in the group. This gave rise to the later error of identifying class with group, so that many had to be perceived before a universal could be achieved, for it was not a true universal but only a group concept. What was valid in Aristotle's thought was that the class concept has some verification in the individual, but not the verification of class. There is something in the individual whereby it belongs to a class. It participates in the reality of the class; it is an imitation of the class reality though in singular fashion. The universal can be predicated of it, though not in its formal sense of class. There is a direct universal, i.e., the universal of predication of singulars, but it is a faulty analysis to suppose that the reflex universal, i.e., the true class concept, is formed by reflection on the direct. Reflection on the direct only shows that prior to predication the mind has already seen the so-called reflex universal, but has seen it rapidly and without pause. It was here that Thomas supplemented the Aristotelian doctrine of intrinsic form with the non-Aristotelian doctrine of extrinsic forms which are of course the true universals, the non-existent exemplars of all existents. Since these do not exist except fundamentally in the infinity of God, they cannot be achieved experimentally, for they cannot act, since action follows only on existence. *Universale ante rem, in re, post rem.*

Intuition

The scientist has a comfortable satisfaction on reflecting that unlike the philosopher, he deals with stuff into which he can get his hands. There is nothing mystical about it. There it is and everybody can see it and touch it.

Of course, the deeper the scientist goes, the less this is true. For a long time he was dealing with the ether, which he has finally rejected because he thinks now that it is not there. But he thought it was there for a century. He has difficulty with his quantum waves, and he certainly cannot get his hands into them; however, there is a convincing ring to all his statements, because a fairly definite image can be formed.

The philosopher is not in so fortunate a position. He cannot give us precise images. He is forced to speak in myths, and myths always carry with them the air of the fanciful and unreal. Yet it is far easier to *understand* what the philosopher is talking about than the objects of the scientist's discourse, in spite of the clipped images that he presents. Just because the philosopher uses intuition does not render his speech less intelligible, but more so. The word intuition only means the recognition of meaning. The meanings he deals with are not the meanings of words, which are conventional signs, but the meanings of things which are realities. Both the scientist and the philosopher suppose that reality is meaningful, and the philosopher deals exclusively with this meaningfulness. Thought is essentially the grasp of the real through meaning. This is clear to all, even the most unreflective thinkers. The eternal question, "what does it mean?" is put by all men, though they may put it in its more valid form "what is it?" The scientist never answers this question at all, at least it is not his intention to answer it. He describes for you the process of the manifestation of meaningfulness, without ever touching meaning at all. He is the depicter of events; he is not entirely unlike the painter and the poet.

This is why philosophy is always older than science. Man

gropes for meaning. Sheer pictorial description, no matter how formalized, is not sufficient for his curiosity, which is nothing but his natural dynamism.

Definition of philosophy

Philosophy is the thought discipline which proceeds from the real considered in terms of meanings, achieved spontaneously by the mind in its search of the real, to the rational erection of a hierarchical system of principles derived from the meanings achieved, in order to give the ultimate understanding of reality in as far as it is assimilable by the natural human mind.

The word "hierarchical" merely means that the principles will be interrelated and interdependent, so that all subsequent principles rest on the previous ones and consequently all depend on the first.

This definition is not meant to be better than others given by other philosophers. It is given with the supposition that it is saying the same that all philosophers have said, but that it is more intelligible in the context of our time.

Philosophy and science

In our dealing with science we saw that it was a valid and fruitful discipline. Philosophy is no less valid, for man searches for meaning in reality. It is no less useful, though its utility is not so pragmatic. Philosophy does not help us to make things; it only adjusts us luminously to the world in which we live. Adjustment is no small boon.

Philosophy in its purest form is clearly metaphysics. The attempt of some philosophers to give us a philosophy without metaphysics is just delusion. These philosophers in reality try to make of philosophy a mathematics which will be at the disposal of science. Most theoretical scientists are philosophers in this sense. However, they are not true philosophers, for they are not independent of the rules of science as the framework for their investigations. Philosophy is beyond the framework of science, and its framework is so ample that it can include the study of science itself, which science can hardly do to philosophy. The logical positivist's attempt to make philosophy a book-keeper and accountant of science is simply the rejection of the validity of philosophy *in se*. Such a rejection is chimerical. It cannot be done. Even science needs philosophical justification and this means that science supposes the existence of philosophy as a distinct discipline.

The existence of the mathematical discipline confuses the whole issue. As it stands, it is neither physical science nor philosophy. However, it belongs to the world of philosophy just as the method of any activity belongs to that activity. Mathematics is only the rational process rendered explicit. It is at home both in science and philosophy because both of these disciplines use reason in their work. However, the justification of mathematics depends on meaning, and meaning is the object of philosophy, and not of science. Mathematics can prescind from this dependence because it is a practical scheme, a practical science as Aristotle and Thomas taught with reference to one small field of mathematics, the Aristotelian logic. This makes mathematics easily serviceable in science. However, the meaningfulness of mathematics will only be derived from philosophy. Mathematics is method rather than thought object. Philosophy deals with the real as it is and not as it must be achieved, and therefore we cannot restrict philosophy only to the consideration of method. Method is justified by its purpose, as all activity is justified by its end.

The real problem is whether philosophy can be anything else but metaphysics. Is "natural philosophy" possible? Is a "rational cosmology" a meaningful term? Is a "rational psychology" meaningful?

Natural philosophy and rational psychology exist. However, is this existence real or apparent? The reason why the question can be posited is that philosophy deals with meaning and cannot jump from meaning to existence. Yet cosmology and psychology deal with the existent. They are not merely systems of the possible, but are also systems of the existent.

It is here that we meet the great difficulty in the matter of cosmology and psychology. Philosophy deals with meaning and not with experience; however, we noted in our analysis of the thought processes that only experience can indicate the existent. Metaphysical intuition only finds meanings, which of themselves are non-existent. Empirical judgment is the thought process that achieves existence. It would seem, therefore, that on our own analysis either the existent cosmological and psychological are the objects of science exclusively, or at least that philosophy can speak of these things only as given by science. Philosophy would, in this latter position, be not unlike mathematics, which does its work independently of science, but in such a way as to be available to science without any existential commitment a priori, and without any imperatives levied on science.

The solution of this difficulty must be sought. We can be sure that there will be a solution, because if there is none, then we are forced to admit that existence can be organized without meaning, or at least without meaning that is certainly proper to it. Such a conclusion simply flies into the face of the dynamism of all human knowledge, which is a search of meaning. The mind cannot approach the existent except as meaningful. The meanings offered by science are free, for the empirical is organized by physical concepts which are frankly presented as constructs, and not truly apprehensions of meaning in the objects themselves.

The key to the solution is possibly in the field of "common sense." Science certainly begins there, for there is no other place to begin. Philosophy also begins there, for the same reason. Both disciplines refine their proper object according to their distinctive methods, but both began at the same point. If the starting point of science is valid enough for it, the selfsame starting point is valid for philosophy.

This fact, however, already indicates the limits of a philosophical cosmology or philosophical psychology. In our dealing with "common sense," we found it valid only for the grosser aspects of the experimental real. Philosophic cosmology, then, can only deal with the grosser aspects of the empirical. It cannot deal with the objects derived from disciplined experience, because this is the field of experimental science. Philosophy can never be a short cut avoiding the work of science, nor can it be a substitute for science because its own methods will not give the valid object of science. In like manner, science which takes over the metaphysic in "common sense" has no right to make short cuts so as to avoid the philosophic labor, nor can it be a substitute for philosophy.

The grosser aspects of the experimental are given with "common sense" and concerning these, philosophy can, and should, talk. There is here an undefined field and for that reason serious error can arise. Much of the cosmology of Aristotelian thinking was derived from a supposed experience which was never critically purified by a more refined and methodical experience. The result was that an image of the real was sketched and, with this taken as true, all blank spaces were filled in by metaphysical thinking constructed *ad hoc*. The result was an image of the world that was so far removed from the objective existence of the world that the first essays of science showed it up to be fanciful myth rather than valid explanation. Certain Aristotelian principles brandished as indestructible swords proved to be paper blades. "Nature abhors a vacuum," "action at a distance is impossible," "whatever is moved is moved by another," do not measure the existential real in the simple forms in which they are presented. There is in these principles a metaphysical base which when expressed is mere tautology. As instruments for the understanding of experience they are not valid because they were expressed to explain a geocentric world as presented by "common sense."

The errors of the earlier cosmologist should be a help to his modern counterpart. He must avoid the impulse to dictate to experience. He should deal with those meanings which are inseparable from any and all experimented reality. He cannot deal with the meanings that are proper to refined scientific experience because science gives only constructed meanings for such experience, and only scientific experience can deal with this field. Nor need the metaphysician say that he can control scientific thinking by holding up the lamp of logic. The scientist has taken good care of this by using mathematics, which is a fuller light than the Aristotelian logic. The scientist does not need the philosopher to help him and vice versa, the philosopher does not need the scientist to help him. Being human beings and actuated by identical drives, they must not forget the other's existence and they can be helped mutually, but this is the help given by different workers in the common effort to find all truth.

  It is impossible to define a priori what is the field of the existential which is the object of philosophic cosmology and philosophic psychology. However, some things can be validly studied. The meaning of extension certainly is a legitimate investigation for the metaphysician because the scientist deals with the extended as given by "common sense." Along with extension the philosopher can deal with such realities as time, space, and motion. The problem of the "continuum" is still a metaphysical problem even though the problem of the topological continuum has been solved by Cantor and Dedekind in mathematics. However, when the philosopher deals with the existent continuum, he must not suppose that bodies are continuous according to some image, Aristotelian or otherwise. He had better let the image be made by the scientists. Likewise, to make sure that he has not been led by "common sense" to go beyond the legitimate field of "common sense," let him by all means study what Cantor and Dedekind have to say about the continuum in order to refine his own notion of the continuum so as to rid it of any element that is not proper to it. He must bear in mind what physics has to say in order to be sure that he is not talking nonsense. After all, if he is talking about the existent, empirical science must be a negative norm.

The meaning of matter is also a legitimate object of philosophic investigation. This meaning is given on the "common sense" level and then carried over into the scientific field. The scientist deals with matter, and therefore he must use the "common sense" notion of matter to find his object. This pre-scientific matter is also at the disposal of the philosopher. He need have no fear that he will soon be dealing with a matter that is not the one that interested the scientist, because the scientist deals only with matter, and all he knows is matter, and what this matter is, at least by implication, he takes from "common sense." The philosopher, in dealing with this same matter, is dealing with the same thing as the scientist, but from a different point of view. The scientist will make an image which will depict matter as experienced; the philosopher will analyze the meaning which will make matter understandable. These are different tasks, and the image of the scientist does not contradict the meaning analysis of the philosopher because the philosopher uses his image as a stimulus to understanding, while the scientist uses his image as a stimulus to experience and practical control. A hydrographic map does not contradict a population-density map because their colorings and figures are different. They are mapping out the same area under different aspects.

Especially in the question of the world as world does the philosopher have a task. The meaning of such a notion, the legitimacy of such a notion as descriptive of the experimental manifold, the prime origin of such a world, the necessary laws of action in such a world in terms of causality, are all subjects that a scientist cannot discuss at all. The philosopher can and must.

As can be seen from this rapid survey, a rational cosmology is not only possible but necessary. It must bear in mind that it is not science but something different—philosophy. It is not experimental. The fact that it deals with the existent is a datum which it derives from "common sense." It can be helped by science to avoid error, but it cannot be helped by science to come to its conclusions.

Today we need a cosmology more than ever. Unfortunately only the scholastic philosophy deals with it and in dealing with it, it is hampered by the framework imposed on it by the cosmological thinking of the Aristotelian framework of this discipline. The result is that nothing basically new has been done for over four hundred years. Other philosophies eliminated cosmology, turning over the whole field to the scientist, with the result that scholastic philosophy was not aroused by newness from within or from without. Kant denied the possibility of a rational cosmology. The scholastics mixed up new science with old cosmology and the result is that the whole study is pretty dismal. We note that today there is an unrest in this entire field. Vincent E. Smith's book, *Philosophical Physics*,[9] tried to get away from the hodge-podge by a return to a cosmology as erected by John of St. Thomas. This will give us a purer cosmology but hardly a modern one. But from a purer cosmology a more modern and legitimate one may come.

This same unrest is felt in the field of science. Men like Eddington and Jeans really did some metaphysical investigation, a fact that was thrown up to them by scientists who saw that such work was not "scientific." But Eddington and Jeans entered into this field because there was a felt need for it. If their work was not as metaphysically solid as it might be, we must remember that their training did not fit them into the philosophical tradition. Their lack of training gave them one great advantage: they dealt with the problems in modern terms.

As we have proposed philosophy and science, it is evident that there is a wall of separation between them. This separation is not to be understood as the separation of fighting dogs

---

[9] New York: Harper & Brothers, 1950.

which, if they meet, will certainly tear each other apart. It is the separation of delimitation so that each will be able to do his work better. The two disciplines can work in harmony, but in the harmony of parallel activity and not of dependence. Science should illuminate the philosopher, just as philosophy should illuminate the scientist.

Sapientia

There arises, however, one great problem. If philosophy is separated from science, then whence shall we find the discipline that can make a synthesis of all the known? It was perhaps for this reason as well as because of the complexity of science that Ernst Cassirer denied that an Aristotelian or Thomistic synthesis is possible in our day. This denial, however, hardly proves the point at issue, but seems rather to be a consolatory anesthetic for the pain felt by all that the synthesis is not being made. Great syntheses are rare in the history of culture, and they were always the products of extraordinary genius. Perhaps the lack of synthesis merely means that the necessary genius has not arrived.

Aristotle's synthesis was possible because philosophy and science were fused into one thing. Such a fusion was not a good thing, but it facilitated the task of synthesis. After Aristotle a new discipline was framed, that of theology, which was fused with philosophy. Aquinas separated the two, but did not separate science from philosophy, and produced a synthesis without worrying much if it was theology, philosophy, or science. Aquinas was not as universal a genius as Leonardo da Vinci or Galileo Galilei. His knowledge of mathematics does not seem to have been profound. His notions of history were vague. Experimental science was quite unknown to him, though Albertus Magnus did some of this work. Yet he did make the last satisfactory synthesis. Cassirer's appeal to the complexity and rich plurality of scientific work does not prove that a synthesis cannot be made. A synthesis by definition is more than an orderly résumé. It must be an essential reduction, which will omit the multiplicity of accidents, cut through a vast amount of irrelevant detail, by-pass illegitimate accretions, which accretions will promptly wither because of the manifestations of their needlessness.

Such a synthesis will not be the fruit of science, nor of philosophy, nor of mere theology. It will be the product of *sapientia* and not of *scientia*. No single discipline can produce it, because disciplines abstract their object from the total field of knowledge and never consider the object from all points of view. It may take on the dress of philosophy or theology. In Thomas it was offered in theology. In Aristotle it was offered in philosophy. It will always be an insight into the concrete culture of a period and will require a spiritual resonance with all that is being done by the spirit in a given time which will enable the investigator to see the whole steadily. Perhaps the reason why we have no such synthesis today is because there is no integration in our modern culture, which is in inner conflict because of divergent tendencies. A certain basic unity of vision is necessary in society in order to produce a synthesis of what it sees. Whether we are approaching such a unity is not clear at the moment, though there is more unity present than is often suspected.

At all events, the dynamism of the great synthesis will not be from any one discipline. It will be produced by a balanced use of all thought processes of a serene spirit of open vision that will be able to pierce through the superficial manifold of the findings of different disciplines in order to reach the point of view where multiplicity will be swallowed up in unity. The font of such a vision let us call with Thomas, *sapientia*. If one wishes to call it philosophy in a fuller sense of that word, there is no need to quarrel. It merely supposes that philosophy is understood differently from the historic discipline so labeled. Philosophy as historically manifest is a thought discipline. *Sapientia* is not a thought discipline but the achievement of perfect balance in the use of all thought processes. It supposes a personal sanity of the highest order. It requires the well-rounded man. Asceticism, balance, and easy adjustment to the real in all its phases are needed for him who has *sapientia*. A theologian might add that grace alone could produce all these requisites, and certainly grace cannot be eliminated from *sapientia*. At all events, though thought disciplines can be taught, *sapientia* cannot be taught at all. It is the flower of right thinking, and the flower is the product not only of the organism, but of the soil, temperature, moisture, and fecundization from beyond. We can hope for the synthesis that will be the flower of *sapientia,* but we cannot really teach men to produce it. Seeds can be planted and nurtured, but the flower will be a product that cannot be controlled, because the precise plant that produces it and how it is produced, is really unknown.

Bibliography

Epistemological Theory through the Ages

Plato, *Timaeus, Gorgias,* and *Theaetetus,* in *The Dialogues of Plato,* 4th ed., ed. Benjamin Jowett, 4 vols. New York: Oxford University Press, Inc., 1953.

Aristotle, *Organon* and *On the Soul,* in *The Works of Aristotle: The Oxford Translation,* eds. J. A. Smith and W. D. Ross, 12 vols. New York: Oxford University Press, Inc., 1910-52.

Augustine, *Soliloquium, De Ideis,* and *Contra Academicos,* in *Opera Omnia.* Paris: J. P. Migne, 1841-77.

Thomas Aquinas, *On Being and Essence (De Ente et Essentia),* trans. G. G. Leckie. New York: Appleton-Century-Crofts, Inc., 1937.

————, *Summa contra Gentiles,* Bk. 2, chaps. 46-78 and Bk. 3, chaps. 38-63, trans. Fathers of the English Dominican Province. New York: Benziger Brothers, Inc., 1923-1929.

Francis Bacon, *Advancement of Learning and Novum Organum,* ed. J. Creighton. New York: Colonial Publishing, Inc., 1900.

René Descartes, *Discourse on Method,* trans. A. D. Lindsay. New York: E. P. Dutton & Co., Inc. (Everyman's Library), 1934.

Baruch Benedict Spinoza, *On the Improvement of the Understanding* in *The Chief Works of Benedict de Spinoza,* trans. R. H. M. Elwes, 2 vols. New York: Dover Publications, Inc., 1951.

Gottfried Wilhelm Leibniz, *Discourse on Metaphysics* in *Philosophical Writings of G. Leibniz,* trans. Mary Morris. New York: E. P. Dutton & Co., Inc. (Everyman's Library), 1934.

John Locke, *An Essay concerning Human Understanding,* ed. A. C. Fraser, 2 vols. New York: Dover Publications, Inc., 1959.

George Berkeley, *Of the Principles of Human Knowledge,* ed. T. E. Jessop. London: A. Brown & Sons, 1937.

David Hume, *Enquiries concerning Human Understanding and concerning the Principles Of Morals,* 2nd ed., ed. L. A. Selby-Bigge. Oxford: The Clarendon Press, 1951.

Immanuel Kant, *Critique of Pure Reason,* 2nd ed., trans. F. Max Müller. New York: The Macmillan Company, 1934.

John Stuart Mill, *A System of Logic,* 8th ed. New York: Longmans, Green & Co., Inc., 1929.

William James, *Pragmatism and Other Essays.* New York: Meridian Books, Inc., 1955.

Edmund Husserl, *Ideas: General Introduction to Pure Phenomenology,* trans. W. R. Boyce Gibson. New York: The Macmillan Company, 1952.

Marvin Farber, ed., *Philosophical Essays in Memory of Edmund Husserl.* Cambridge, Mass.: Harvard University Press, 1940.

G. E. Moore, *Philosophical Studies.* Patterson, N. J.: Littlefield, Adams & Company, 1959.

George Santayana, *The Realm of Essence* in *Realms of Being.* New York: Charles Scribner's Sons, 1942.

———, *Scepticism and Animal Faith.* New York: Dover Publications, Inc., 1955.

John Dewey, *The Quest for Certainty.* New York: Minton, Balch & Company, 1929.

———, *How We Think.* Boston: D. C. Heath & Company, 1933.

———, *Logic, The Theory of Enquiry.* New York; Holt, Rinehart and Winston, Inc., 1938.

———, with A. F. Bentley, *Knowing and the Known.* Boston: Beacon Press, 1949.

Bertrand Russell, *The Analysis of Mind.* New York: The Macmillan Company, 1921.

———, *Mysticism and Logic.* New York: Doubleday & Company, Inc. (Anchor Books), 1957.

———, *The Problems of Philosophy.* New York: Oxford University Press, Inc., (Galaxy Books), 1959.

———, *An Inquiry into Meaning and Truth.* New York: W. W. Norton & Company, Inc., 1940.

———, *Human Knowledge, Its Scope and Limits.* New York: Simon and Schuster, Inc., 1948.

Moritz Schlick, "The Future of Philosophy" in *Basic Problems of Philosophy,* 2nd ed., ed. D. J. Bronstein et al. Englewood Cliffs, N. J.: Prentice-Hall, Inc., 1955.

Rudolf Carnap, *Meaning and Necessity,* 2nd ed. Chicago: University of Chicago Press, 1956.

Alfred Ayer, *Language, Truth and Logic.* New York: Dover Publications, Inc., 1953.

———, *Philosophical Essays.* New York: St. Martin's Press, Inc., 1954.

———, *The Problem of Knowledge.* Baltimore: Penguin Books, Inc., 1956.

Charles Morris, *Signs, Language and Behavior.* Englewood Cliffs, N. J.: Prentice-Hall, Inc., 1946.

Ernst Cassirer, *Essay on Man.* New Haven, Conn.: Yale University Press, 1944.

———, *Language and Myth,* trans. S. K. Langer. New York: Dover Publications, Inc., 1946.

————, *The Problem of Knowledge: Philosophy, Science and History since Hegel*, trans. William H. Woglom and Charles W. Hendel. New Haven, Conn.: Yale University Press, 1950.

Ernest Nagel, *Sovereign Reason*. Chicago: The Free Press of Glencoe, Illinois, 1954.

Modern Scholastic Epistemologies

Balmes, Jaime, *El Criterio (The Art of Thinking Well)*, trans. W. W. McDonald. Dublin: M. H. Gill & Sons, Ltd., 1882.

————, *Filosofia Fundamental (Fundamental Philosophy)*, trans. H. W. Brownson. New York: William H. Sadlier, Inc., 1856.

Maréchal, Joseph, S. J., *Le Point de départ de la métaphysique, Cahier 5, Le Thomisme devant la philosophie critique*, 3rd ed. Paris: Desclée, de Brouwer et Compagnie, 1944.

Riet, Georges van, *L'Épistémologie Thomiste*. Louvain: Editions de l'Institut Supérieur de Philosophie, 1946. (A history of recent Scholastic epistemology.)

Söhngen, Gottlieb, *Sein und Gegenstand*. Munster, i. W.: Aschendorffsche Verlagsbuchhandlung, 1950.

Steenberghen, Fernand van, *Epistemology*, trans. M. J. Flynn. New York: Joseph F. Wagner, Inc., 1949.

Current Survey Manuals

Beck, Lewis White, *Philosophic Enquiry*. Englewood Cliffs, N. J.: Prentice-Hall, Inc., 1952.

Black, Max, *Problems of Analysis*. Ithaca, N. Y.: Cornell University Press, 1954.

Brennan, Joseph G., *The Meaning of Philosophy*. New York: Harper & Brothers, 1953.

Feigl, Herbert and Wilfred Sellars, *Readings in Philosophical Analysis*. New York: Appleton-Century-Crofts, Inc., 1949.

Hospers, John, *An Introduction to Philosophical Analysis*. Englewood Cliffs, N. J.: Prentice-Hall, Inc., 1953.

Houde, R. and J. P. Mullally, eds., *Philosophy of Knowledge: Selected Readings*. New York: J. B. Lippincott Co., 1960.

Philosophy and Science

History of Science

Dampier, W. C., *A History of Science and Its Relations with Philosophy and Religion*, 4th ed., rev. and enlarged. New York: Cambridge University Press, 1949.

Hall, A. R., *The Scientific Revolution 1500-1800: The Formation of the Modern Scientific Attitude.* New York: Longmans, Green & Co., Inc., 1954.

Lange, F. A., *The History of Materialism,* trans. E. C. Thomas. New York: Harcourt, Brace & World, Inc., 1925.

Sarton, G., *Introduction to the History of Science,* 3 vols. published to date, published for Carnegie Inst. of Washington. Baltimore: The Williams & Wilkins Co., 1927-1948.

Taylor, Frank Sherwood, *A Short History of Science and Scientific Thought.* New York: W. W. Norton & Company, Inc., 1949.

Wolf, A., *A History of Science, Technology and Philosophy in the XVIth and XVIIth Centuries.* New York: The Macmillan Company, 1935.

———, *A History of Science, Technology and Philosophy in the XVIIIth Century.* New York: The Macmillan Company, 1939.

Modern physics

d'Abro, A., *The Rise of the New Physics,* 2nd rev. ed., 2 vols. New York: Dover Publications, Inc., 1953.

Blanchard, C. H. and others, *Introduction to Modern Physics.* Englewood Cliffs, N. J.: Prentice-Hall, Inc., 1958.

Born, Max, *The Restless Universe,* 2nd rev. ed. New York: Dover Publications, Inc., 1957.

Broglie, Louis de, *Physics and Microphysics.* New York: Pantheon Books, Inc., 1954.

Einstein, Albert, *Relativity, the Special and General Theory,* trans. R. W. Lawson. New York: Hartsdale House, Inc., 1947.

———, and Leopold Infeld, *The Evolution of Physics.* New York: Simon and Schuster, Inc., 1938.

Heisenberg, Werner, *The Physical Principles of Quantum Theory,* trans. C. Eckart and F. C. Hoyt. Chicago: University of Chicago Press, 1930.

Lindsay, R. B. and H. Margenau, *Foundations of Physics.* New York: Dover Publications, Inc., 1957.

Rogers, E. M., *Physics for the Inquiring Mind: The Methods, Nature and Philosophy of Physical Science.* Princeton, N. J.: Princeton University Press, 1959.

Theory and method

Blake, R. M., C. J. Ducasse, and E. H. Madden, *Theories of Scientific Method: The Renaissance through the Nineteenth Century.* Seattle: University of Washington Press, 1960.

Born, M., *Experiment and Theory in Physics.* New York: Dover Publications, Inc., 1955.

Broad, C. D., *Scientific Thought*. Patterson, N. J.: Littlefield, Adams & Company, 1959.

Burtt, E. A., *The Metaphysical Foundations of Modern Physical Science,* rev. ed. New York: Humanities Press, 1951.

Carnap, R., *The Unity of Science,* trans. M. Black. London: George Routledge & Sons, Ltd., 1934.

Churchman, C. W., *Theory of Experimental Inference*. New York: The Macmillan Company, 1948.

Cohen, M. R., *Studies in Philosophy and Science*. New York: Frederick Unger Publishing Co., 1959.

————, *Reason and Nature,* rev. ed. Chicago: The Free Press of Glencoe, Illinois, 1953.

Cooley, H. R., D. Gans, M. Kline, and H. E. Wahlert, *Introduction to Mathematics: A Survey Emphasizing Mathematical Ideas and Their Relations to Other Fields of Knowledge,* 2nd ed. Boston: Houghton Mifflin Company, 1949.

Dantzig, T., *Number, the Language of Science,* 4th ed. rev. New York: The Macmillan Company, 1954.

Duhem, P., *The Aim and Structure of Physical Theory,* trans. P. Wiener. Princeton, N. J.: Princeton University Press, 1954.

Einstein, A., *Essays in Science,* trans. Alan Harris. New York: Philosophical Library, Inc., 1953.

Eddington, A., *The Nature of the Physical World*. New York: The Macmillan Company, 1929.

————, *Philosophy of Physical Science*. Ann Arbor, Mich.: University of Michigan Press, 1958.

Frank, P., *Foundations of Physics, Encyc. of Unified Science,* I, 7. Chicago: University of Chicago Press, 1946.

————, *Philosophy of Science: The Link between Science and Philosophy*. Englewood Cliffs, N. J.: Prentice-Hall, Inc., 1957.

Heisenberg, W., *Physics and Philosophy: The Revolution in Modern Science*. New York: Harper & Brothers, 1958.

————, *Physicist's Conception of Nature*. New York: Harcourt, Brace & World, Inc., 1958.

Jeans, J., *The New Background of Science,* 2nd ed. New York: Cambridge University Press, 1934.

————, *Physics and Philosophy*. Ann Arbor, Mich.: University of Michigan Press, 1958.

Joad, C. E. M., *Philosophical Aspects of Modern Science*. New York: The Macmillan Company, 1932.

Jordan, P., *Physics of the Twentieth Century,* trans. E. Oshry. New York: Philsophical Library, Inc., 1944.

Kaiser, C. H., *An Essay on Method*. New Brunswick, N. J.: Rutgers University Press, 1952.

Kemeny, J., *A Philosopher Looks at Science*. Princeton, N. J.: D. Van Nostrand Co., Inc., 1959.

Margenau, H., *The Nature of Physical Reality*. New York: McGraw-Hill Book Co., Inc., 1950.

Maritain, J., *The Philosophy of Nature*. New York: Philosophical Library, Inc., 1951.

Mises, R. von, *Positivism*. Cambridge, Mass.: Harvard University Press, 1951.

Pearson, K., *The Grammar of Science*, rev. ed. New York: E. P. Dutton & Co., Inc., 1937.

Planck, M., *Where Is Science Going?* trans. J. Murphy. New York: W. W. Norton & Company, Inc., 1932.

———, *Philosophy of Physics*, trans. H. Johnson. New York: W. W. Norton & Company, Inc., 1936.

Poincaré, H., *Science and Hypothesis*. New York: Dover Publications, Inc., 1952.

Reichenbach, H., *Modern Philosophy of Science: Selected Essays*, trans. Maria Reichenbach. New York: Humanities Press, 1959.

Samuel, H. L., *Essay in Physics*. New York: Harcourt, Brace & World, Inc., 1952.

Standen, A., *Science Is a Sacred Cow*. New York: E. P. Dutton & Co., Inc., 1950.

Stebbing, L. S., *Philosophy and the Physicists*. New York: Dover Publications, Inc., 1958.

Sullivan, J. W. N., *The Limitations of Science*. New York: The New American Library of World Literature, Inc. (Mentor Books), 1952.

Weiner, P. P., ed., *Readings in the Philosophy of Science*. New York: Charles Scribner's Sons, 1953.

Werkmeister, W. H., *The Basis and Structure of Knowledge*. New York: Harper & Brothers, 1948.

———, *A Philosophy of Science*. New York: Harper & Brothers, 1940.

Whitehead, A. N., *The Concept of Nature*. Ann Arbor, Mich: University of Michigan Press, 1957.

Whittaker, E. T., *Space and Spirit*. Chicago: Henry Regnery Co., 1948.

———, *The Beginning and End of the World*. London: Oxford University Press, Inc., 1942.

———, *From Euclid to Eddington: A Study of the Conceptions of the External World*. New York: Dover Publications, Inc., 1958.

Readings Related to the Whole Subject

Amerio, F., *Epistemologi Contemporanei*. Torino: Società Editrice Internazionale, 1952.

Bergson, H., *An Introduction to Metaphysics,* trans. T. E. Hulme. New York: G. P. Putnam's Sons, 1912.

——, *Creative Mind,* trans. M. L. Andison. New York: Philosophical Library, Inc., 1946.

Bochenski, I. M., *Contemporary European Philosophy,* trans. D. Nicholl and K. Aschenbrenner. Berkeley, Calif.: University of California Press, 1956.

——, *Die Zeitgenossischen Denkmethoden.* Bern: A. Francke, 1954.

Lonergan, B., *Insight, A Study of Human Understanding.* New York: Philosophical Library, Inc., 1956.

Maritain, J., *The Degrees of Knowledge,* trans. under supervision of G. Phelan. New York: Charles Scribner's Sons, 1959.

——, *An Introduction to Philosophy,* trans. E. I. Watkin. New York: Sheed & Ward, 1933.

——, *Reflexions sur l'intelligence et sur sa vie propre.* Paris: Desclée, de Brouwer et Compagnie, 1924.

Martin, W. O., *The Order and Integration of Knowledge.* Ann Arbor, Mich.: University of Michigan Press, 1957.

Rousselot, P., *The Intellectualism of St. Thomas,* trans. J. E. O'Mahoney. New York: Sheed & Ward, 1935.

Simon, Y., *Introduction à l'ontologie du connaître.* Paris: Desclée, de Brouwer et Compagnie, 1934.

Smith, V. E., *Philosophical Physics.* New York: Harper & Brothers, 1950.

Index of Names

Index of Topics

117